MW00450701

CAMPFIRE TALES
& OTHER LIES

JACK BARRY

Publisher's Information

EBookBakery Books

Author contact: jbarry1141@gmail.com

ISBN 978-1-953080-16-5

© 2021 by Jack Barry
Cover photo by Jack J. Barry, III

ALL RIGHTS RESERVED

ACKNOWLEDGMENTS

Thanks to I. Michael Grossman whose energy and professional wizardry guided us fearlessly through the bookmaker's swamp. I also want to give a special thanks to my sons James, Jack and also his wife Pat, who volunteered their time and patience to turn my words into my life. Thanks to Linda Langloise and the Wakefield Guild and Sue Berman and the URI OLLI Writing Group for their challenging prompts and encouraging critiques. And finally, thanks to my Primary Care Physician John O'Leary who kept me healthy, happy, and laughing despite my many bad habits these 30 years.

DEDICATION

This book is dedicated to my wonderful wife, Gerry.

FORWARD

Every now and then I'll hear a tune or catch a scent of something that conjures up an entire era of my life. When that happens, I depart the land of "Now" and float down the river of "Then" only to find a few sandbars still above water and wonder what might be rusting away on the bottom. Writing helps this dredging. Some of it might be junk, but it's my junk. In many of the stories I try to reflect my voice of past times. This can be mortifying and politically incorrect, but it reflects life's lessons learned.

A few years ago, my kids urged me to write up the stories I told around the campfire at our family campsite in New Hampshire (cover photo of actual family campsite fire). I suspect it was an attempt by them to gather material that might help in the defense of their own sins and misdemeanors. Although I started writing for my kids, I now write to see the smile, hear the laugh, see the knowing nod when someone reads one of my stories. I now write to chase that moment of almost physical pleasure when I find that lightning word or phrase. It doesn't matter if the lightning is not in the same sky as Mark Twain's.

Over the years, many folks have come to enjoy the stories (some even believed them). While I use the campfire circle to tie stories together, the stories go well beyond what I told my now adult kids those many years ago.

So grab a s'more and welcome to my campfire.

Contents

IRELAND

Leaving Tralee 1923

The train pulls at a tearful departure
wheels push faster with each hasty goodbye.
A young girl sits with her back to the future
missing a rainbow as she watches her past disappear.
Oh! There'll be plenty more rainbows
one for every sad story I'm told.
Fine beads of mist etch the train window
gathering and re-gathering
kaleidoscope patches
of bright field green against grey Irish rain.
Church window shards sliding away
not a saint to be seen
darkness comes to wipe clean the slate.
"Goodbye Old Ireland, I'm going to Cork!"
She's off to America, "the next parish over."

1

MOM

The author Jack J. Barry and son Brendan Connor Barry walk
near the Three Sisters, Ballyferriter, Ireland. 2015.

MOM'S HOMECOMING

From my earliest memories there was an altar in our bedroom. It was
the Virgin Mary in her blue and white robes, palms turned outward,
guarded by plump cherubs holding our rosary beads and scapulars. An
old postcard leaned against Mary's inviting hands. It was a photo of
the Three Sisters. Three promontories standing firm against western
Ireland's fierce North Atlantic, hovering above a handful of farms on
the rough edge of Ireland's west coast. The profile of those dark hills in
that postcard was imprinted on me, etched in my soul. Waiting.

Three Landers sisters were born in the shadow of those hills: Josephine (Jo) the oldest and smartest; my mother Bett, the loyal, hardworking middle child; and Catherine, the childless, good times, good fun, youngest. It was a place of hard weather and hard living—no electricity, phones, cars, or even running water.

The Three Landers Sisters, Josephine (right), Catherine (center), and Bett (left). 1934.

One by one, in their early twenties, the three sisters left their home to make their way in America, the oldest Jo first. They followed a well-worn path born of the 1845 potato famine and the hundred-year Irish Diaspora that followed. As my mother along with hundreds of thousands of immigrants would say: "Goodbye Old Ireland, I'm going to Cork!" From Cork, Bett crossed by boat, made it through Ellis Island, and on to Hartford, Connecticut.

Each sister helped the next get started in their new country, America. Their first jobs were as maids and cooks in wealthy homes. I remember my mother still speaking with a hint of awe about sticking a cord in the wall and feeling the clothes iron get hot.

In 1971, at the age of thirty, I scraped together enough money to take Bett back to Ireland. She had not been back in almost fifty years. A bus took her and me over the rise between the town of Dingle and the hamlet of Ballincolla. As the sun sank into the sea, casting long rich shadows, the Dingle peninsula spread before us, pointing west, pointing to America the next parish over. The Three Sisters rose before me exactly where they always were. Only this time, instead of old postcard sepia, a verdant green. This time it was real. I had been here before; though it was my first time in Ireland.

Bett smoked a pipe, used Parodi cigars for tobacco, loved boiled pig's feet, had a rich brogue, and used Gaelic to discuss grownup matters with her sisters. She never made much of her Irishness. It was just her way. I took these things for granted just as I took her unconditional love for granted. This was the beginning of a trip where I found my mother, who she was before I was. I discovered a life, a place, a race that was part of me without my knowing.

This was a place of beauty and magic—a place of the open door, close community, and extended family. People had to be there for each other in order to survive. And they did survive—they flourished. Their wealth was in their language, their stories, their music, their laughter. This is not the idyll of the romantic American returning to his imagined roots. The harsh unforgiving sea, barren land, long dark winters, dreams lost, and the curse of drink were there all right. But those cold facts only made the magic all the more magical.

During our stay at my uncle Tomás and his wife Kate's house in Ballincolla, I learned much about my mother and even some things about myself. Back in her first home, her real home, my mother was in full stride. All her childhood friends were now in their late sixties, early seventies. Uninvited and unannounced they would come to Tomás' and Kate's home, take a seat by the turf fire and start right in with a story or song in Irish from the good days, the days of their youth.

Often they would forget part of the story or song. My mother would finish it. She started many of her own which would trigger another round of memories and laughter. That kitchen was often crowded. The locals liked my mother. The fifty years in the states had not much changed her. She spoke Irish like the day she left. She was one of them. Her return triggered a wake—an Irish wake to celebrate their youth gone by. They said Bett's memory of her youth in Ireland was still fresh in her mind because it was frozen fifty years back, but perhaps it was not frozen at all but was a small flame kindled, a soft breath on the coals to help warm each day in her new land so far from home.

SACRIFICE

Bett's passport photo. 1972.

My mother Bett returned to Ireland twice over ten years to care for her mother Mary Connor who was stricken with pleurisy and died in 1934. Bett was the middle sister of three. It was expected that each sister would take turns returning to Ireland to care for their ill mother and help brother Tomás on the farm. However, Josephine (Jo), the oldest, was engaged and soon to be married, Catherine, the youngest refused to return to Ireland, so, the burden fell back on dependable Bett.

What made her sacrifice particularly painful was that her first language was Gaelic. She could barely read or write English and was terrified that she might never be able to return to America. (In 1950 Bett proudly won her American Citizenship.) After the death of her mother, Bett did return to America. But, the final insult came when her sister Jo chose Catherine over Bett to be her Maid of Honor in 1935.

Bett married John Barry (my dad) in 1937. It was clear that Dad had a severe drinking problem. He also was seven years younger than Bett which, back then, was viewed as a weakness. She called this "The time of my breakdown." She never talked about her courtship with my father. Most likely, because it was so sad. I began to understand why it took her 40 years to return.

But looking back over all these years, this sadness could not have stayed sad for very long. My sister Pat and I took for granted that our aunts, uncles, and cousins loved us. In order for us kids to enjoy being with our cousins, Bett would have had to forgive Jo and Catherine for the lifelong anguish she endured. Bett would forgive but could never forget. She sacrificed ten years of her youth and swallowed the role of the "Poor wife" to give her children the best she could. Bett displayed a persistence and resiliency that served my sister Pat and I well. We never felt deprived.

For the most part, Bett worked as a domestic worker cleaning houses in Hartford's suburbs for about $4 a day. She used to take me with her before I started school at the age of four. I can still remember some of the houses and their people. I could sense at the age of four that Mom was proud of me. When work dried up she applied for State Aid, and appeared before Harford's Catholic charity The Diocesan Bureau. These handouts caused great anxiety for Bett. She was afraid a case worker would find out she worked while collecting State Aid. I have no information as to how the Hartford version of the Diocesan Bureau might stack up against writer Frank McCourt's depiction of the cruel treatment his mother Angela received in Ireland. For Bett, appearing before the Hartford Bureau was torture, but her kids came first. In 1950, domestic workers were finally allowed to participate in America's Social Security program. That certainly helped us.

Of the many traits Irish immigrants brought to America, fine conversation—preferably in a bar—may well be number one. A close second is the culture of the open door. Neighborhood kids, friends, friends of friends, schoolmates, even grownups all contributed to a lively stew of humanity at our house. If things got tight, Bett just threw more potatoes into the pot. The open door changed the way we saw our universe. It was a universe made up of people not buildings. A universe always changing, often challenged.

*Thanks go to my sister, Pat Sweet for digging out many of these sad details from long ago.

Tigh Tomás

Uncle Tomás and Aunt Kate in their old tigh. 1979.

This is a story of houses, houses that served as home for many generations of Landers in Ballincolla, Ireland. This story includes the home of Uncle Tomás and Aunt Kate. It includes the "new" house that Michael Landers built on the foundation of Tomás's now defunct house. It also includes the ancient shed that must have sheltered many Landers over countless years.

My uncle Tomás Landers was not directly related to the Landers next door. You would have to go back a few generations to find a common ancestor. As my mother used to say "We had the same name but you could marry them you know." Related or not, the Landers next door made Tomás part of their family, especially after Kate died in 1978. But, even with their love and care, time took its toll on Tomás and his old house. He died in 1993 at the age of 93. He was all dressed up the day he died with his dancing shoes on, waiting to celebrate Eileen Landers's wedding.

I owned Tomás's old house because Tomás and Kate wanted to give it to me. I insisted on paying them at least a nominal fee. In 2013 Michael Landers contacted me about buying Tomás's now deserted house. I charged him the same nominal fee.

Gerry and Jack in Michael's rebuilt home in same spot as Kate and Tomás. 2015.

In 2015, I'm back in Ballincolla in Michael Lander's new house admiring the new fireplace and looking at a long familiar photo. Ballincolla is a hamlet outside of Ballyferriter at the foot of the Three Sisters where the Landers, including Bett, grew up. In the first photo above that's my uncle Tomás Landers and his wife Kate Higgins Landers. It was taken by local photographer Aodán O'Connor for a newspaper article about home heating back during the 1970s OPEC energy crisis. The local newspaper was looking for old timers to photograph for the article. No doubt, Tomás and Kate were well qualified. The kettle hanging from the crane over the turf fire speaks to this.

I discovered the ancient shed when I first came to Ballincolla in 1972. The Landers kids back then had urged me, the Yank, to peek into an old stone shed connecting Tomás' home with the Landers home. Their sly smiles should have forewarned me as I turned the latch and stepped into the darkness. Lying there on her side taking up almost the entire length of the ancient shed was a sow nursing a string of newborn piglets. Until that moment, my American city boy's pig expectations leaned a bit more toward Walt Disney's hairless, pink, and clean Porky Pig. This mother pig definitely needed a shave. But, there was another surprise. There was a small but well-built fireplace at the far end of the shed. It told me that long ago, that humble shed was someone's home—maybe a Landers's.

Looking back, I knew Michael Landers would take much better care of the place than I ever could, an ocean away. It did not take me long to see that this new house was built with great love and care, reflecting the intelligence and persistence of those who built it. And now, in 2015, I stand in the new house in front of the new fireplace built over the old one—a beautiful, welcoming home for generations of De Londras to come.

Ancient shed before rebuild.

Jack with Michael Landers at his house—built over tigh Tomás. 2015.

CENTRALITY

Let me tell you a bit about my uncle Tomás. For Uncle Tomás, Ballincolla was the center of his universe and any variation of the Irish language was a foreign language for him. Beyond traveling to the "hub" of the ten-mile-away town of Dingle, he only ventured further once, on a forty mile trip to Tralee. He lived for 93 years, most all of them in the house in which he was born. Today, many folks would view this confined life a punishment, but perhaps it explains his longevity too. He died with his dancing shoes on, waiting for the wedding of his niece Eileen Landers to start.

Tomás was in his teens when a fishing boat went down off the Blasket Islands within sight of his home. The crew was comprised of French and North Africans. Tomás was struck by the fact that most of the crew was barefoot and the bottom of the Black sailors' feet and palms of their hands were pink—at least he would always mention it when telling the story. From that day on, for Tomás, all foreigners were Frenchmen.

It's Saturday night. I'm in my Uncle Tomás's house in Ballincolla when a young man comes with the message. A Yank, my friend Ned Cosgrove's brother Jim is looking for me in Ballyferriter, about a five-minute drive from Tomás's house. Although Tomás is well into his eighties there is no question he will "help me" find the Yank. With only three bars in town it's easy to find Jim. Tonight the bars are open until two AM, well past the regular 11:20 PM bar closing, because there's a big Gaelic Athletic Association (GAA) football tournament in town.

The GAA is one of many groups in Ireland working to preserve the Irish language and culture. It is a hard fight. The gravitational pull of English is powerful and constant, made even more difficult by the fact that much of Ireland never spoke Irish and the English did their best to suppress it. Old Norse Vikings named Wexford and Waterford. Today, the Gaeltacht, an area where Irish is the native tongue, clings to narrow strips on the west coast of Ireland like mussels clinging to its rocky shores. The tide is relentless. Before Independence in 1922, Irish football and hurling clubs were used to form underground political organizations. Playing the native sports and speaking the native language nurtured the resistance. Today the GAA games are still used to stem that tide.

The street and bars are crowded with young men dressed in bright team colors, all speaking Gaelic, singing Irish songs, and knocking back pints at a rapid pace. Their eyes light up when they see Tomás in his well-worn cap and dark wool coat. Here is a true old timer who spoke Gaelic before he spoke English. He learned it at his mother's side, not in school, not because it was a political statement, not because some jobs require it.

The pints pile up in front of us. Tomás' presence elicits more than Guinness. Gaelic songs are sung. Gaelic backs are slapped. Gaelic tears of happiness and belonging freely flow. We three have one grand time. Especially Tomás. When the bars finally close and Jim goes back to his hotel, we head back home. It's quiet. It's well after closing, we're both exhausted.

"Did you enjoy the evening Tomás?"

"I did!"

"Those lads were grand weren't they?"

"That they were…for Frenchmen."

I'm glad the lads from Galway weren't around to hear that.

BALLYFERRITER

A Moment in Time

It's a slow November day, a handful of locals gather in Donal Kane's pub in Ballyferriter to knock back a pint or two and do what we Irish do best—talk. Too many full pints of Guinness are lined up in front of me, bought by old timers who still remember my mother fifty years back. I'm trying to figure out how to deal with these foaming Guinness tributes when I hear a keening flat nasal cry turning to melody, as the hum of soft Kerry accents give the room back to the music. The music is coming from a young man who looks to be in his twenties. You can see by his ruddy face he spends most of his time working in the hard western Ireland winter wind. His voice is as clear and sweet as his old Gaelic lament will allow. When the last note is sung the room stays silent for a moment… Finally an old timer turns to the young man, tips his hat "Stout lad!" Others nod. Then, along with the young man, they return to their talk. The silence lasts but for a moment. It will be with me forever.

Donal Kane

A few days later, I find myself back in Kane's pub. This time, no music. Rather a different kind of music. This time the place is empty except for the owner Donal Kane. But, he more than fills the place for me. He's spent most of his life in this village—a church, school, post office, general store, creamery, and three bars. He is well versed in matters of the world, has a great wit, and best of all, remembers my mother well. So, instead of an assembly line of free pints for me, Bett's son, I am nursing one pint on the house. Donal tells one story after another about the history of this place and its people. He is proud of his heritage and more than happy to share it with this blank slate Yank who carries the blood of this place. I'm beginning to learn a bit more about who I am, who my mother was.

He tells me about the big Hollywood movie they made here last year—*Ryan's Daughter*. He tells me how the story never could have happened the way it was in the movie with all that adultery and so forth. He tells me how Trevor Howard best known for his roles in *Brief Encounter* and *Third Man* was a dope addict, pervert and worst of all, snooty. How everyone loved John Mills who performed in 120 films and won Best Supporting Actor, how they built an entire village back behind Clogher (a hamlet a few miles west of Ballyferriter) then knocked it down when the movie was done. Donal thought the movie village would be good for tourism.

It was about two in the afternoon. The November sun was well on its way west. Donal said "Ah! But, you must see all this for yourself. Come along!" He took off his apron, locked the doors of his pub and took me on a tour of the Dingle peninsula until it got dark. My education was just starting!

This is a poem I wrote for Donal from one of the stories he told me about seeing the famous plane, the Spirit of Saint Louis, in 1927 as it made its maiden journey across the Atlantic. Considering that the Dingle Peninsula is the western most point of western Europe and Donal's land is in the western most area, there is a high likelihood he was the first person to view the plane as it flew over Europe.

The Kerry Shore - 1927

The rough Atlantic charges stone sentinels.
Mighty rollers stunned sparkling white
on their run to the west reaching Kerry shore.
Chewing on the past.
Spitting back bones clean and white,
a Viking blade,
a cross from the Armada,
a cigarette case from a German sub.
But, this time it's the future that comes.
Silver wings born on the early morning breeze.
The cows hear it first.
They run in circles, kicking at nothing,
skittish, fearful.
Futures will do that.
The drone grows louder,
rising to a scream in the ears of young Donal Kane.
In terror, he falls to his knees in the pasture,
but looks up in time to be the first in Europe to see.

"The Spirit of Saint Louis" heading for Paris,
flying into the future. 1927.

GROWING UP

2

MY FATHER

My father, John J. Barry. 1979.

This photo of my father is the only evidence I could find that he ever existed. It was taken at my wedding in 1979 where the booze flowed freely. He gave a weak try at our standard shouting match before he passed out. As for his looks, craggy comes to mind. You could see by his face that he led an interesting life.

I do remember his hands. They were big and strong. He played semi-pro football in Springfield, Massachusetts but got injured. He also had a shit-eating grin that I inherited from him. But, the thing I remember most was his hair. He was called Red and he was. This was cool because at the time there was a well-known wrestler called Wild Red Barry. I could tell the kids at school my father was Wild Red and I wasn't lying—really.

EARLY DAYS

My Dad grew up in South Boston and on Hungry Hill in Springfield, Massachusetts. That's about as Irish as anyone who's never set foot on the *Ould Sod* can get. Despite his Irish bona fides, he didn't much like the newly arrived Greenhorns from the old country. I suspect they didn't much like this Yank narrow-back who was competing for one of their own—my mother.

He played the harmonica, a big double hole Hohner, He liked Stephen Foster songs. His favorite song though was Big Rock Candy Mountain. He rode the rails during the Depression where, among other things, he learned the difference between a hobo, who wandered the country and was willing to work for his food, and a bum. Dad put himself in the bum category when explaining this hierarchy of sobriety and trustworthiness to me. He spent much of his adult life drunk on the streets or drying out either at home, or in jail. In later years jail was replaced by VA homes. He served in the Army Air Force in WWII. He stayed in the States and worked on B29 bomber planes. He never spoke much about it. The only story I ever got from him about the Army is when he did a week in the brig for setting off a fire alarm while he was drunk.

When Dad was in high school, his father was killed by falling bricks at a construction site in Boston. This changed his life far more than the Great Depression or all the "No Irish Need Apply" signs. He and his brother attended Latin High School. But I don't know if that claim was really Boston Latin. It didn't matter. Dad had to quit school to help support the family. Dad was smart. His older brother Justin was smarter. Justin remained in school. Dad often talked of running into a nun after he quit school who said to him "Oh John! Why can't you be like your brother Justin?" Dad told that story often enough to make me realize it changed his life. However. By the time I was a teen I suspected alcohol was just Dad's bullet of choice. He had a strong bent for self-destruction—if not alcohol, than drugs, gambling, whatever. Dad never had a job as important as was the booze, other than trying the job of hauling fully filled ash barrels to the ash truck in his forties. After a week of exhaustive work, he got a hernia and quit.

THE PHONE CALL

I'm eight years old running down the street in Hartford's North End. The night is still warm. Neighbors are out on their stoops catching a little breeze and news of the day. I wish the street was empty. It's late and I feel their stares. "A little kid shouldn't be out at this time of night, especially running in pajamas with shoelaces flopping and all. White boy too."

I'm heading to the fire station to call the cops on my father because we don't have a phone. He's drunk and under the window again yelling up to let him in. But my mother knows better. He'll yell, then beg, then cry. He's sorry. He'll try to be good. But we know he won't. He's got enough booze in him to be falling down but not enough yet to pass out. This means he'll stay up all night harassing us. But, sooner or later, fearing some neighbor will play the righteous asshole and start a fight, we let dad in. We close our bedroom doors and ignore his yelling, his promises, his tears. Then he'll start cooking, anything to smoke us out. This we can't ignore. It's not the burnt food that worries us, it's the grease fire and broken glass.

This is a regular routine every time he comes back to dry out and every time he takes off again, he winds up like a wild goose running on water to take off. It's worse when he brings friends home. Some feel bad when they see us but most just keep on drinking. Like this is all normal.

The fireman makes the call to the police station and leads me into the fire station kitchen. He tells me to wait till the cops come to take my father, sits me at the table and gives me a Coke. I check out the slide-down pole. This is pretty neat!

THE TURNING TIDE

About eight years later things change a bit. The city bus is coming to bring me home to the North End in Hartford. I'm sixteen, working summers and weekends for Mack McCarthy, a landscaper my mother knows from the old country. I have just finished a ten-hour day raking leaves. I never knew how hard ten hours of raking was. Getting on the bus, I reach in my jeans pocket for the quarter bus fare. Pain explodes from my wrist. Damn! Is it broken? When I get home I just want to take a bath and go to bed. When I awake it's like coming up from the bottom of a murky pond. Then I hear my father's voice and the pond clears fast. I run down the stairs and yell at him to quit the crap and go to bed. My father runs up the stairs at me. I push him back. He falls down the stairs, lands on his back, grabs a chair and starts to swing it at me. I grab the chair in his hands and my mother screams "Don't hurt him! Don't hurt him." At that moment my father and I both realize my mother is screaming at me, not him; not that she cares about protecting him, but to keep me from doing something I'd be sorry for. He lets go of the chair, grins that shit eating grin and says "You didn't think I would did ya?" I tell him to go to bed. He does.

EBB TIDE

My experiences with my father were not all bad. In fact, he was a good influence. When he was sober he was a good guy. Unfortunately this was less than half the time—gone for months, back for weeks. But, drunk or sober, he took me places like Willy Pep's gym in downtown Hartford, wrestling matches, the Sportsman Show, and of course, to his gin mills. I would usually get a lot of slobbering attention. A guy with a pet monkey hung out in one bar. He always gave me an apple. I didn't like the apples but was surprised I didn't much like the monkey either. It seemed to me like we were part of the same act.

THE GRIN

I inherited that shit eating grin from my father. I'm glad none of my kids was so inflicted. It's a real grin but, sometimes it slips into a smirk. Like those skeletons in biology class hanging there grinning away when they obviously got nothing to grin about. Over the years many nuns, priests, cops, and the like swore that they would wipe that smirk right off my face. This only made me grin more. This likely made the nun more inflamed, the priest more abusive, and the cop more fucking profane. The cycle starts all over again until sometimes, my jaw muscles lock up and involuntary tears begin to flow. Adults interpret the tears as a white flag, the first step toward submission to the realm of adult authority. The first step toward redemption. If they could look past the tears, they would have seen a big "Fuck You." The cops were the easiest. They usually had much bigger fish to fry than mess with our tadpole misdemeanors. As the grin cycle escalated, I learned new swear words or new ways to use old swear words from them.

My grin problems occasionally carry over to this very day. The worst times are with my wife Gerry. I love Gerry ferociously. She sees the grin as a total and absolute sign of disrespect. The more important the issue, the more I grin, and the more she feels disrespected. Not good. Not good at all. I have considered plastic surgery or maybe Botox, but I'm not sure how I would eat. Perhaps I'll just put bag over my head when we have something important to discuss.

LESSONS LEARNED

Many years ago, a famous news reporter Mike Wallace interviewed the son of the infamous Jewish gangster Mickey Cohen. The son said the best advice his father ever gave him was that "to get respect you have to give respect." My father, when he was around and sober, gave me respect. He often made me cry but he also showed me how to laugh. My latch key upbringing gave me freedom and independence. I had to figure out most things for myself—a mixed blessing. My life in the projects paradoxically gave me twenty years of stability amidst the daily earthquakes. It provided a Ph.D. on the human condition. My neighbors' thriving shortcomings helped me see my own. Finally, luck has given me good genes, good health, and all the great things mentioned above. I also believe the world is a better place because there were times I did not get caught. I take no credit in what luck has brought me. But I do take credit for being wise enough to enjoy it while I can.

By some accounts, I should have turned out to be a sexually conflicted, substance abusing, small time B&E man. I grew up on welfare in a single parent home. In a housing project in the Black part of town. There were few male role models. Growing up in a changing neighborhood showed me early on that life was seldom black and white. Dysfunction, self-destruction, and professional victimhood abounded. I was not only exposed to it. I was immersed in it. But, that account ignores some fundamentals.

Looking back, I think I did manage to get a few things right. As near as I can figure, here's why. My mother's unconditional love gave me security, optimism, and the ability to love (if not the wisdom to profess it to loved ones early and often). Her hard work gave me a strong work ethic and perseverance. I learned about loyalty from her everyday sacrifice. I also believe the world is a better place because there were some times I did not get caught. I take no credit for being wise enough to enjoy it while I can.

The fact that my father wasn't around much—and when he was, seldom stayed long enough to become "head of the household"—gave me the freedom to grow up at my own pace. If you can't win by the Man's rules, you make up your own. In my old neighborhood, as in all too many neighborhoods today, values were upside down. For example, we were proud the day we found out that cops would not come into the project alone. In our world, we single parent kids felt sorry for kids who still had fathers living at home. I can vividly remember a spat I had with Rumpy Raposa. Rumpy was a good kid and the spat was just a kid-sized discharge of nastiness that would dissolve by morning. Later, after the spat with Rumpy, as I was walking past Rumpy's house, his father throws open the window, points his finger at me and screams, "Hey You!... You an altar boy?"

"Yeah?"

"You sonofabitch you!" With that he slams the window shut.

I did think he had a point but the tone was scary. I felt sorry for Rumpy. His father wasn't leaving anytime soon. So, although I never learned to make layups off the correct foot, I never had an adult male relive his youth through me or try to protect me from the un-protectable. I believe my kids also benefited from this hands-off approach. I was their father, not their playmate. They got security, love, and respect but, unasked for advice, not so much. They tell me now, the best advice I ever gave them was "Never break more than one law at a time." As I found later in life, this helped me navigate the upside down values.

LAST DAYS

I'm in St. Francis Hospital in Hartford, Connecticut. I can't tell if Dad is delirious or a school yard wise guy. He's imitating his Indian doctor's accent, indulging in a bit of softcore racism, getting his last shots in the school yard. Trying to look like he's in control. I figure he's scared. He should be. They amputated his leg yesterday and called me to tell me he doesn't have much time left—it's emphysema. He smokes right up to the end. I haven't heard from him for several months, and last I knew he was doing okay at the VA home in Rocky Hill. Seeing him in the hospital he flashes that shit eating grin. It no longer works. It's his last dance.

3

FRIENDS & NEIGHBORS

As with most eastern cities, Hartford, Connecticut experienced tremendous changes during the 19 years I grew up there—1941-1960. These changes were driven by black migration from the South, white flight to the suburbs, and later, migration from the Caribbean islands. By the time I left Nelton Court, I was a white minority among minorities.

Nelton Court in Hartford's North End was built in 1940. It housed 120 apartments in fourteen two-story red brick buildings. These barracks-like buildings were laid out in neat orderly rows for folks whose lives were far from neat or orderly. Every time I go back, my childhood universe shrinks. The brick and mortar neighborhood was bulldozed a few years ago. It has risen again, brand new buildings waiting for new tenants to create their own universes. Now, my old neighborhood is no longer bound by Main Street to the east and Acton Street to the west. It's located somewhere between my east and west ears and, on occasion, spills over to light up my frontal lobe.

So, I bid farewell to Raincoat Red who had a special trench coat filled with inside pockets to carry the half pints he sold after hours.

Farewell to Alice From Across who introduced herself to her new neighbors in pajamas "Hi! I'm Alice from across." One day, she called the cops on her husband Wayne then used a frying pan to protect him from those very same cops.

Farewell to Spaghetti, a lanky 6'4 140 pound, debonair black man, always impeccably dressed. He usually appeared one drink away from collapsing into a bony heap of bespoke pinstripe. On his daily trip downtown he would flip a silver dollar up the street, walk up to it and flip it again until he reached the bus stop. Who knows why? Every time he bent over was a gravity defying feat.

Farewell to Jungle Jim Leahy who came to town with the circus in 1946 and broke windows in order to spend the winter in a warm jail cell. Legend has it that he threw a brick through the window of the campaign headquarters of Connecticut Governor Abraham Ribicoff. When the cops started to question him, he said "Here, I'll show ya," and threw a brick through another window.

Farewell to Minnie Scatta and her sons Subby and Jughead who got into their share of mayhem but are mentioned here because I like their names.

Farewell to all those folk who shaped my universe, and, for good or bad, helped shape me. You will meet more of them as you paddle along with me.

WORMS

Mrs. Turner was the blackest person I ever knew and maybe the oldest, skinniest, and nicest. She went catfishing every Saturday morning by the Connecticut River down past Fish Fry Street. One summer when I was about eight or nine, she gave me and Butchie Bavarskis a job. Butchie was a tall skinny kid with a nasty laugh. He never knew his real father and his mother was seldom without a boyfriend or a drink. Besides being a lot bigger than me, he was three years older. Every Friday night me and Butchie would catch night crawlers for Mrs. Turner, a penny a worm. We'd usually get ten or fifteen worms. For us that was good money. As the summer went by, things dried up. The Night crawlers stayed home. We were desperate. We tried digging and caught hell for wrecking the little grass that was left in the project. We poured water on the ground from milk bottles. It didn't help. Week after week no rain, no worms no money! Just dust!

Then one Friday I woke up to a hard rain. It rained all day. As if on command, the downpour stopped right at dusk. Night crawlers were everywhere. Me and Butchie got our flashlights and started scooping worms like crazy. We even recruited little kids to help. We needed more containers. Quart milk bottles replaced pint jars. Altogether we must have had at least three gallons of night crawlers. It was glorious; but, the pitch in our mother's voices calling us in for the third time told us time was running out. "In a minute, Ma!" We knew when our mothers saw our treasure they would just dance around the kitchen in joy. We figured at least a thousand worms. Maybe more! Ten Bucks! We hurried to Mrs. Turner's house to cash in. "Oh! I'm sorry boys but I got all the worms I need right here from my own lawn. All this rain. They just jumpin' outa the ground!" She saw the shock, the despair. "You know boys, I think Mr. Black could use some worms and he just might be payin' two cents a worm." Goodbye misery, hello Mr. Black! Two cents a worm! Twenty Bucks!

Mr. Black lived at the end of the unit. Like Mrs. Turner, he was also real black but the main thing was he had the widest nostrils of any man on earth. This was no lie, because we'd spy on him clearing his nose, slinging snot one nostril at a time out his window while we hid under giant leaves we mistakenly called skunk cabbage. He never would have let loose if he knew we were hiding in those jungle weeds. He was a nice man. But the lights were out in Mr. Black's house and our mothers' calling had reached that final shrill "Right this minute!" pitch. Tomorrow! Mr. Black! Twenty Bucks!

I didn't sleep much that night. Butchie scrounged all the bottles and jars he could find and kept the worms in his house. He was older than me so I didn't quite trust him. It didn't occur to me that it might be hard to sell worms in the middle of the night. I guess when you're sitting on a treasure you start to think a little different.

The next day I wake up late. The sun is already hot in spite of the clear blue sky the storm pulled in from Canada. Butchie carries jars and bottles of worms out of his house, lining them up near the sidewalk like they're New York Yankee World Series trophies. Like me, Butchie also has galoshes on because even though it's sunny and hot there's still plenty of water around from yesterday's rain.

But, there's a problem! The worms are making this white gooey foam like stuff. It's disgusting – somehow dirty in a strange way. We know it has to be stopped. We pour some water in a jar full of worms. They squirm even more, make more "stuff" and start to drown. Next Butchie tells me to get some towels. He knows better than to take any from his house. That's how you are when you're older. I get the towels without my mother seeing. We start rolling worms on the towel. No good. We pour some worms on the towel and throw the worms in the air like a trampoline. Also, no good. We spread the worms on one towel, put the second one on top and start gently patting it. We begin to understand that towels are not the solution.

Butchie leans back to rethink our approach, putting his hands behind him. When they touch the sidewalk he quickly pulls them back, then grins. You might not be able to fry an egg on that sidewalk but it's pretty damn hot. I never saw a worm jump before. It's a worm-like jump but these poor little cusses can really move. But then, they curl up and die, baked into little black strings right on that sidewalk. Lucky we have a lot of worms! We figure we'll put up with the white stuff after all.

There's also a change in plans. Butchie's mother's boyfriend says there's a store on Front Street in the Italian neighborhood near the Connecticut River that buys night crawlers a nickel apiece. Hotdam! Fifty Bucks! Not only that, but he's headed downtown and can drop us off within a few blocks of the store. We find a box, pour all our worms in, and are on our way. When we get downtown, we notice the bottom of the box is getting wet and beginning to sag. On the way to Front Street we find a box even better than the one we had. Perfect! Luck is with us.

Butchie's mother's boyfriend can't remember the name of the store but tells Butchie about where it is. We walk down Front Street, past Saint Anthony's church until we get to a store we figure has to be it. It has lots of strange stuff I never saw before—boxes of zucchini, broccoli, melons displayed outside, heavy smelling cheeses and ominous sausages hanging in the window, beautiful cans of olive oil stacked like a pyramid, an entire wall of cages holding chickens and rabbits. But, no sign of worms, no sign about worms and the men inside don't look all that friendly. I'm not sure they speak American.

I keep waiting for Butchie to go in. He tells me to go in and ask the guy if he buys worms. What the hell? I mean, he's the older one. He should do all the talking, besides, I got the towels and will probably catch a few whacks from my mother.

Just then a little girl comes out of the store. "Hey! Hey little girl… Do uh …they buy worms in there?"

"Are you crazy?"

It's insulting the way that little girl wrinkles her nose and shouts CARAYZEEEE. But, she leaves no doubt in our minds that this store does not buy worms and probably not one Italian in the entire city does either. But hey! There's still Mr. Black! Twenty bucks still sounds pretty damn good.

The bus driver jokes as we get on the bus, "What ya got in the box boys, Good Humor ice creams?" Lucky it's early afternoon. The bus is almost empty. We go all the way to the back, put the box on the floor between two seats and sit there in a semi daze. We're on the Barbour Street bus which turns left off Main Street onto Capen. You can get off the bus at the corner of Capen and Main or ride a few more minutes and get off at Barbour and Nelson. Six of one; a half dozen of the other. I'm thinking we get off at Barbour. But, as the bus rounds the corner onto Capen, Butchie jumps up, yanks the stop buzzer and grabs the box.

I can still hear those worms slopping out of the suddenly left behind bottom of that box. It's like slow motion in the movies. We look at each other, consider all options. This takes less than a second. Jumping over the still oozing heap, we run off the bus. We run and run. We run in those heavy galoshes on this hot day. Surely my lungs are going to bust open. I think I'm gonna die. We run past the project in case the bus driver, cops, FBI, our mothers might be on our trail. We double back and hide in the skunk cabbage. Still no sign of Mr. Black. We don't care.

No Other Sound

I can hear that sound still, sixty-eight years later. The sound of Rosalee Testadura's grandmother's head hitting the sidewalk. A soft sound that went straight to my stomach.

I was sitting on my stoop in the project, alone, because I was mad at my buddy Bobby. Yesterday, he hit my shoulder with a hammer right where I just got a vaccination. So, I was playing kamikaze bombers where you stick the sharp end of a two inch thorn into a live Japanese beetle butts and fly them around until they run out of gas and the buzzing stops. It's not so much fun playing kamikaze by yourself.

It was July, temperature in the nineties. I watched Rosalee's grandmother slowly trudge up the hill. Puddles of silver heat shimmered off the black street. Rosalee's Grandmother wore a black wool scarf, black wool coat, black wool dress, long black stockings, and black lace-up shoes. I was six or seven. I knew she was a witch.

She made this trek up the hill almost every day. She came to see her daughter Sarah, Rosalee's mother. Sarah had the bad luck of once being beautiful, young, and falling for the wrong guy. The wrong guy was supposed to be a big shot in the mob. I didn't know whether or not that was true, but he did wear a big shot suit with a vest and all the few times I saw him.

Looking back, Sarah was usually drunk by noon, spending her lost afternoons bewildered, wondering whatever happened to that once beautiful young girl, and whatever happened to that long gone wrong guy. Even to this young boy, it was almost painful to catch a glimpse of her beauty buried beneath disappointment and surrender. Rosalee had her mother's good looks. She was a good kid too. So we didn't make fun or anything even though her mother was a drunk and her grandmother was a witch.

The witch was coming closer up the hill, closer to me. I pulled a foot long grass stem with a feathered seed head from some weeds. We usually threw them like little spears. And, that's what I did. I threw it right at the witch. Now, the witch was at least twenty five feet away, and the grass spear flew about three feet. The witch stopped, slowly turned toward me and raised her arm. I knew a curse was coming, I couldn't move. But, I got lucky. She keeled over. I'll never forget the sound of her head hitting that concrete sidewalk. What made it worse, there was no other sound. Nothing! I ran into the house, and slammed the door shut. They never came for me. I never saw her again. I guess they knew she was a witch.

The Hole

Some folks never learn. Freddy Cooper was in a hole. He was also in great pain. The last thing he wanted to do was call for help. He remembered the last time he got caught and he never lived that down. Back then he was running from a cop who spotted him trying to break into Ozzy's TV Land. He could hear the cop huffing and puffing right behind him. At twelve years old Freddy knew he could outrun this fat-ass cop. That's when he looked back and ran into a low hanging branch—flat out, knocked him out. It didn't take long for that story to make its rounds but it took forever for folks to forget. Some still call him Sleepy.

But now, he finds himself in an eight-foot hole with what feels like a broken leg. He's deep in soupy Connecticut red clay at the construction site where they're punching Interstate 91 through downtown, right past the Hartford Police Station. And, it's raining, cold hard rain. How did Freddy get himself in this mess? Here's what happened.

Once again Freddy was into a bit of B&E. This time Lou Dubrutski's grocery store. Lou's store by the way was right next door to Ozzy's TV Land and had even less good stuff inside. And, once again, he got caught. A paddy wagon was conveniently nearby so the cops chucked Freddy into the paddy wagon along with the usual cargo of drunks, brawlers, and wife-beaters. When they got to the police station, the driver beeped for the guard to raise a large iron gate. He drove into the courtyard and rousted the handcuffed prisoners out of the paddy wagon. The gate clanked slowly up. Freddy didn't have time to think. He figured he was still faster than any cop and definitely skinnier. He dived for the gate, rolled under it with inches and seconds to spare and ran. He was fast. He was fast even with handcuffs on. The cops weren't so fast, no matter what swear words they used. The gate continued its slow descent, clanked when it hit the ground, then slowly started right back up. By the time the cops raised the gate and got out to the street Freddy was nowhere in sight.

Freddy could hear them swearing, swearing at the rain, swearing at the red clay, swearing at each other, but mostly swearing at Freddy. Freddy knew. He knew he had to yell to the cops for help. He hoped his leg would get better, but he knew the story would last forever.

Carrying on Without Him

When I first saw him I wondered what he was doing out in the middle of Main Street deep in the Black part of town. He definitely looked white bread among the Black faces checking him out from the sidewalk: blond, crew cut, creased khakis, white short-sleeve shirt with plastic pocket protector, narrow tie, horn rim glasses.

I was on the back of Art Romano's 1957 Indian Tomahawk bike. I didn't have a driver's license back then. Didn't get one until I was twenty-two. So, on a hot summer night Art was my escape out of the housing project where I lived the first twenty years of my life. I met Art at the Hartford State Technical Institute—a forerunner to what we now call community colleges. He would come down to the city and take me for rides on the back of his bike. I loved those rides—the wind in my face took me away. Took me into another world. Sometimes we would head back to his hometown Suffield, Connecticut. We would stop at a drive-in hangout for local kids. There were girls. White girls! Complaining about how boring Suffield was. Say what?!

We had just passed this guy walking in the street when I heard the bang. I always thought it would be a thud but it was a loud bang from the car hood. The thud came when he hit the windshield, rolled over the top of the car and landed in the street. Art did a U turn. We saw a cop running into the street. How did he get here so fast? To me the young man lying in the street looked like a big doll—his arms and legs lying at odd angles. He was dead. That's when I saw the shoes. His shoes. They were on the street right where he got hit. Alone, one in front of the other—quiet, …waiting.

The car that hit the young man was pretty banged up. A middle aged Black man sat in the driver's seat looking stunned. With the sudden appearance of the cop, who now had a dead white man, a guilty Black man, and a growing Black crowd on his hands, a current of prickly energy rippled the hot summer air. Nervous cops and jumpy crowds: a bad mix. I gave Art a let's get the hell out of here look. I don't remember where we went that night.

The next day the *Hartford Courant* had the sad details. Even sadder than I thought. The young man had just graduated from Purdue

University and moved East to work as an engineer at Pratt & Whitney, the jet engine maker in East Hartford. He probably got a little lost and ended up in a small fender bender on Main St. in the North End of Hartford. When the cop came on the scene, he had the young man go into the street and show him what happened. This is a young white man who had just been in an accident, was in a strange place surrounded by a Black crowd. How would he know that these occasions, accidents, fights, fires, whatever, were regular community events? Catch up with your neighbors, check out the street show at hand—just the usual neighborhood bread and circus.

In my mind, that young man should not have been out on that street. He never had a chance. The story of the man that hit him adds to the sadness. About an hour before this accident he was in a minor accident in another town driving home from work. I imagine he had a lot on his mind before he looked up to see a young man with a bright future frozen in the middle of Main Street. The paper played up the back to back accidents as if the driver was a serial killer. It never mentioned what the police protocol might be for sending a person who has just been in an accident onto a busy street. I went in the Army soon after and never found out what happened to the driver, but I am sure his life changed forever just as the young engineer's family back in Indiana had.

In the Army I stole a book of poems out of the Fort Sill library "Nude Descending A Staircase" by X. J. Kennedy. I must have nabbed it because it had the word nude in it (sorry Duchamp). What made me keep the book though was a poem called "Carrying On Without Him" about the shoes of a guy hit by a truck.

One part goes:

> *"Now who would think two leather graves*
> *The clods we rise to don*
> *Could shrug us, no more be our slaves*
> *And footloose carry on."*

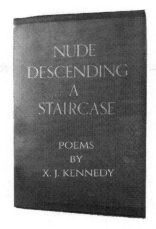

I often think of those summer night bike rides, the young man now forever young, the driver who killed him, and my long journey since. Shoes and lives left behind while I still don't mind to carry on—every gifted day.

A LITTLE NIGHT MUSIC

Freddy's brother Russell worked as the second shift maintenance man at Terry Steam Turbine. Every night near midnight he would walk home singing. I swear, he had the best voice I ever heard. Good as the great R&B ballad man Sam Cooke! In my later years I now fall asleep to church bells in a picture perfect postcard New England village. The church bells sure are nice, but I would take Russell's sweet song anytime. The thing though was that Russell was flamboyantly gay. That's not exactly the words we used back then. He was called a "faggot," a "screaming queen," and worse. Given how most of us saw guys like him, I'm surprised he didn't get beat up or worse. His family probably had a lot to do with that. Tough kids. One brother, Jo Jo, was a professional boxer. To us, that meant his fists were legally lethal weapons—legally the same as a gun.

But I think Russell himself had a lot to do with the fact that most of us actually liked him. It wasn't just his singing either. You see, he was also flamboyantly Christian. He wore a big cross on a chain around his neck. He would sing Ray Charles tunes to gospel lyrics and claim the music came straight from Jesus. Now most folks in the project figured that Jesus forgot about them long ago. But, not Russell! He believed. Really believed. I mean, I believed too, I was even an altar boy. But my belief back then was all about confession, sin, what not to do, when to eat fish, where not to touch yourself. But, with all that failure, despair, and differentness surrounding him, Russell was sincerely jubilant, even ecstatic! Yeah, he believed.

Many years have gone by since I last saw Russell, but sometimes, when church bells toll, I still wonder how he's doing.

FOOD FOR THOUGHT

When I was in grammar school, going home for lunch meant going to Pat Casey's Italian Restaurant because my mother worked cleaning houses across town and my father was not around. Pasqual Cassarino (Pat Casey) was an overweight ex-prize fighter who ran the restaurant and took a few bets on the side. Rumor had it he was connected. Maybe he was, maybe he wasn't. Though we never heard of pasta we really liked Pat's spaghetti, macaroni, and what in Harford were then called Guinea Grinders.

Pat Casey proved to be the real thing when I saw him lay out Diane Steinberg's mother's boyfriend with three short jabs. They fought over some imagined disrespect. In the project you seldom needed much of a reason. The boyfriend was feeling no pain until he caught those punches. Up to then my notion of a grown-up fight was shaped by Roy Rogers. He would knock the villain out with one clean punch that sounded like a Miriam Makeba Xhosa love song (never heard of Makeba? Check out her songs "Click Song" and "Pata Pata" while you're at it). That single punch would put the villain out exactly long enough to allow Roy to sing a song with Dale Evans, or trap the rest of the bad guys in some box canyon.

What Pat did to Diane Steinberg's mother's boyfriend was not like Roy Rogers at all. There was blood, broken teeth, and drool—pure primal domination. It was over fast. It scared us. This was not play. Diane Steinberg's mother's boyfriend just sat on the floor blinking and bleeding. Soon after, he left the neighborhood.

Besides the food, Pat Casey's had a TV stuck up in the corner. My family still didn't have one so anything on the black and white tube was entertainment. This included the Kefauver Senate hearings that shined the light on the Mob in the fifties. I began to look forward to the hearings almost as much as the Wednesday spaghetti special.

Like Pat Casey, Francesco Castiglia "Irished up" his name to Frank Costello. (Yes Costello is an Irish name. My Irish mother pronounced it with the accent on the first syllable.) Frank "the Prime Minister" Costello was a mob boss who controlled a gambling empire across the United States, and enjoyed some political influence. They would show only his hands on TV. But his voice! Now here was a real gangster: smooth, haughty, in control, and best of all, he wasn't scared of no cops. Before the hearings, we were not very political although I do remember the 1948 election. I was seven and got my first taste of political activism. Word was that if Tom Dewey got elected we would have school on Saturdays. We were scared to death. I mean what evil grownup man would want to send kids to school on Saturdays? So we marched around the neighborhood chanting "Truman's in the White House. He will keep us free. Dewey's in the garbage pail where he oughta be." So, with our help along with a late surge in the American heartland, Harry Truman won that election. I sometimes wonder what ever happened to Diane Steinberg's mother's boyfriend.

EARLY MAIL

It was the last day of school. All we had left to do was put fresh brown paper covers on the books we'd leave for next year's first graders, and then we got out early. No more reading, no more books. No more teacher's dirty looks! I ran all the way home. I was five years old. Usually my sister collected the mail when we came home for lunch. She could reach the mailbox easier, but this time, I got home before her, getting a jump on summer vacation. Oh! happy day! Two mail boxes were attached to the front door trim board that separated our apartment, Unit 2A, from our next door neighbor's, Unit 1A. As I straddled the step to reach for the mail our neighbor Mrs. Kirschnitz came out. She was a very nice woman. I liked her. I think she liked me too, but I figured she would leave the project as soon as her husband came home from the war. I mean, she even had a phone.

"Oh, Hi Jacky! Last day of school? I bet you're happy about that!"

"Happiest day of my whole life Mrs Kirschnitz. I got the whole summer off."

She leaned over me. For a minute I thought she was going to hug me or something but she was just getting her mail from the box above ours. "Have fun, Jacky!"

As soon as she closed the door I felt the pain. At first I thought it was a bee sting or something but when I tried to see what it was I realized I could not move my finger. It was stuck in the hinge of Mrs. Kirschnitz door. I tapped on her door window. It took a long, long time for her to come to the door. I tapped again. Maybe she just got a letter from her husband. But she finally pushed back the little curtain on her door window.

"Oh, Hi Jacky. What do you want?"

"The door Mrs. Kirschnitz! The door!"

"Yes Jacky?"

"The door Mrs. Kirschnitz! My finger is stuck in your door!" With that she let out a screech and flung the door open.

A small blob of raw hamburger appeared where the tip of my pinky used to be. All she could do was hold me to her and say "I'm so sorry, so sorry." I was beginning to bleed on her and got a little scared. Luckily my sister Pat who just got promoted to fourth grade came along. When she saw what was going on she ran upstairs and came down with a bunch of toilet paper. "TOILET PAPER?" Now I really got scared. What if my buddy Bobby saw me all wrapped up with toilet paper? But, I held out my hand and let her wrap the toilet paper around and around my hand. At least you couldn't see the blood anymore.

About then, my father who had just come home from the army a few weeks earlier came out. He did not seem as excited as the three of us and asked Mrs. Kirschnitz to call the cops. My finger now was throbbing, but with dad here, I felt a little better. It seemed to take a long time for the cops to come. The cop who came also did not seem too excited. For some reason that made me mad. The hospital was about three miles away and while it too seemed like a long ride, I hoped we would never get there. I thought hospitals were where older people went to die. My father rode shotgun in front with the cop which must have been a first and maybe a last for Dad.

When we finally got to the hospital they put me in a room and had me watch a small blue pill slowly dissolve in a bowl of warm water. Despite the increasing pain, I hoped the pill would never dissolve, but of course, it did. Long after it dissolved a nurse came in and told me to put my hand in the bowl – pinky still attached. Another long wait. Finally a doctor came in. He took my hand in his and said "Hi Sonny Boy. We're going to sew you right up. You'll be as good as new in no time. It might pinch a bit." PINCH A BIT?! The pain almost killed me, and, besides now my whole hand was a sickly Frankenstein kind of blue. I wanted to smack him (I mean the doctor, not Frankenstein). At least I had real bandages instead of toilet paper.

When we left the hospital my father asked me if I wanted to take the bus back home. Couldn't he see my whole hand was blue?

"Could we walk, Dad?"

A pause, "sure Jacky," I was kind of surprised at how agreeable he was. I was still getting used to the idea that he was home and could boss me around. I think he was still getting used to the idea that he was my father. About half way home we passed a tavern "How about a soda Jacky? You must be thirsty"

Jeez! Couldn't he see my hand was still blue! "No thanks Dad." It was a silent, thirsty, and painful walk the rest of the way home. I was thinking maybe I could put a glove on my blue hand. I was glad to get home without being spotted by any of the big kids. I was even glad to see Mrs.Kirschnitz waiting for me. She gave me a big hug and told me we got no mail today.

PARK AVE

I learned a lot growing up in a changing neighborhood. Some good, some bad. When it comes to race, there are two things that haven't changed much: 1) If I was Black I'd be pissed; 2) As a white man, I'll never really know what it's like to be Black.

Mrs. Turner had a large family—good kids. Her husband was called The Reverend Turner. He was always dressed in a black suit and fedora hat. He kept to himself—seemed a little shell shocked from whatever his silent world threw at him.

One winter night a Black man walks into our unit by mistake. Since every unit in the project is identical, it's pretty easy to make that mistake, but even after we point this out to him, the guy is either too drunk or too stubborn to leave—just standing there swaying and muttering. My mother runs out the back door to call the cops at the Kelly's next door. She screams at us to follow but I have a solution. I call out to my sister, "Hey Pat, get Dad's gun!"

Of course we didn't have a gun and hadn't seen Dad in months. When that solution doesn't work, we run to the Kelly's to wait for the cops. By the time a cop comes, the drunk is gone but we still have hope for justice because there's about an inch of new snow. You didn't have to be Sherlock Holmes to catch up with this culprit. All the cop has to do is follow the tracks of this lumbering drunk. About fifteen minutes later the cop returns triumphantly with a kid from our neighborhood—a very sober fourteen-year-old James Turner, The Reverend's son. The cop must have collared the first black guy he saw. You know, suspicious of being suspicious kind of thing. I mean, how many black guys do you know who like to walk around in the snow at night. You can see the cop would really like to nail James and get back to his warm squad car. As he leaves, unable to make an arrest, the cop feels obliged to remind us to keep our doors locked: "Ya don't live on Park Avenue ya know!" Head down, James looks humiliated. I feel responsible for that cop nabbing James, somehow embarrassed to be white, to be part of the cop.

CLOSE SHAVE

Ann is a good looking nineteen-year-old. She doesn't live in the project but has friends here. Her family moved across town after she graduated from high school. So, on her days off Ann sometimes visits my sister Pat. Even though she's taller than me I walk her to the bus stop because it's Saturday night and the streets are getting lively. We have to go past a Black barroom to get to the bus stop. There are a few men hanging outside the barroom drinking from paper cups or small nip bottles discreetly nestled in paper bags. On this particularly warm Saturday evening the crowd's bigger than usual.

As we get closer, we see that men are standing in a ring watching two guys arguing, foreheads almost touching. One guy's a lot bigger than the other. The smaller man steps back, reaches into his pocket and opens a straight razor, a blade sharp enough to shave you, frisky enough to lay you open. The big guy sees the blade, he leans in closer pokes the little guy gently in the chest, he whispers something, turns his back and walks slowly away, like an alpha dog exposing his throat to number two dog, daring number two to mess with him.

The crowd is disappointed about no fight but glad, I think, that there is no razor play to bring the cops. Men start to drift back into the bar. I'm studiously looking the other way trying to not notice what's going on. It doesn't work. I look up. Too late! We make eye contact. His eyes were bloodshot, jaundiced, and impenetrable. He's less than ten feet from us. A few quick steps, he grabs my arm and pulls me closer, his free arm still holding the razor. It's like we're slow dancing. Ann keeps walking down the street as if it's just another nice day here in the city. Very smart move!

Swaying he says almost softly "Hey man! What's goin' on?" I see Ann is okay but I'm staring at that razor. I picture the arc it will take before it slices through my skinny white arm. I think about making some moves. But I know nobody can stop that razor in time. My mind is racing. What should I say to this guy? "Nothin' mister, Nothin's goin' on." I'm thinking Jesus! This is so lame! How can I get through to this humiliated drunk man with a straight razor in his hand? What the fuck can I say?

Big Man calls over. "Hey Leroy! You stop messin' with that boy! You hear?" Leroy keeps his eyes on me. Keeps hold of my arm. Keeps hold of that razor. Some of the guys still outside the bar chime in "Yeah Leroy leave that boy be! C'mon let's you and me have a little taste. On me man!" The crowd starts to cajole. Leroy looks up and down the street as if he can see something we can't see. He lightens his grip, stands a little taller: Taps me on the chest and half whispers "Ya'll git the fuck outta here!" He drops my arm, carefully folds the razor, turns his back to me and slowly walks away. Just like a top dog. Ann catches the bus. I head for home.

4

WORK & PLAY

The earliest job I can remember was when I was about nine years old. I caught night crawlers a penny apiece for Mrs. Turner. She used them catfishing in the Connecticut River down past Fish Fry Street. My first real job at age thirteen was working on a tobacco farm in the Connecticut River Valley. You had to be fourteen to work on a tobacco farm. I was thirteen but my doctored birth certificate said I was fourteen. I realize now that I didn't have to lie about my age to get a Social Security card from the SS man and that the redneck tobacco farmer in the green pickup could care less how old I was. Back then I thought all adults knew the same stuff about you—at least the bad stuff. Social Security man, farmer, teacher, cop, priest, probation officer all belonged to some monolithic adult nation. So I stood there on tiptoe at the SS counter and hoped the Social Security man would not notice the ballpoint blue zero imposed over the regal black scripted number 1 turning 1941 to 1940. I had done this when I was nine going on ten so that I could convince the Boy Scouts of America I was ten going on eleven. So much for trustworthiness.

FASTEST WHITE BOY ON THE BUS

It's 1972 in a station deep in the London Underground this Black guy looks over and smiles at me. Traveling alone increases opportunities for adventure. But right now, I just want to find a place to sleep. I practice the friendly nod and wink I picked up in Ireland. He keeps looking over and smiling. So much for Irish friendliness. Worse yet, he walks over.

A musical Jamaican lilt, "Don't I know you, mon?"

"Uh. I don't think so man."

"Oh! You from the States?"

"Yeah. So I doubt I know you."

"I was in the States once."

"Yeah, it's a big place."

"Connecticut, mon."

"Connecticut! That's where I grew up. When were you there?"

"1954 and 55."

"I lived in Connecticut then but that was more than twenty years ago. I was just a kid."

The friendly Jamaican said "I worked on a tobacco farm Cullman Brothers. I drive the tractor, mon."

"You gotta be kidding. I picked tobacco on Cullman Brothers tobacco farm"

So Maddox Anderson and I let a few trains go by while we poke each other's memory of summers long gone. I even get Maddox who now works in the British Museum to yell *"Git yor oss down dot row, mon!"* which gets the attention of the polite Brits on the platform. At least they were polite forty years ago. I'm sorry that I never asked what he did at the British Museum. We never did figure out how he recognized me but he definitely knew Cullman Brothers. No doubt about it!

About Cullman Brothers Tobacco

I doubt Mr. Maddox would recognize Cullman Brothers today. The farms are gone. The fertile Connecticut River Valley turned into leafy gated communities and big box malls surrounded by seas of asphalt, weathered tobacco sheds turned into family-room wainscoting and frames for Andrew Wyeth prints. Even Joseph Cullman Jr. who began growing shade tobacco in Connecticut in the early 1900s would not recognize it today. Today's Culbro, LLC was formed in 2005 as the private equity investment vehicle of the Cullman family. Cullman introduced popular cigar brands including the Tiparillo made famous by the ad "Should a gentleman offer a lady a Tiparillo?" In 1959 Fidel Castro expropriated US owned tobacco farms and cigar factories in Cuba. Over time the Cullman family diversified, managing and selling many businesses ranging from snack foods to Ex-Lax. And, all this time, I thought the redneck in the green Cullman Brothers pickup truck owned the farm.

About Picking, Dragging Sowing, & Hanging Shade Tobacco

It's 7am and I'm sitting on my ass between two seemingly endless rows of shade tobacco plants. I'm already sweating. This is no surprise. Many years ago, the shade tobacco moguls determined that the red dirt of the lower Connecticut River Valley is just like the dirt in Sumatra, perfect for growing the cigar wrapper leaf that determines what makes a quality cigar. The only problem is that the red dirt is in Connecticut and Connecticut is in frigid New England. This little problem is fixed by covering tobacco fields with a cheesecloth-like material ten feet high covering acres. This keeps the heat and humidity in and any stray zephyr out. On a sunny summer day the wet-bulb temperature is pushing a hundred degrees. People from Sumatra might like it. We kids don't! We, who hump on our asses for eight hours a day picking tobacco by the leaf! There is plenty fainting and malingering. They haul barrels of drinking water out to the fields but the word among us boys is that it's spiked with saltpeter. This potion according to teenage legend, reduces sex drive. This would keep us from messing with sowers working in the sheds. Sowers are girls and women who thread a string through the stem of the tobacco leaf and tie the string of leaves to four foot laths (thin boards). The laths are then hung in the shed by hangers. Hangers work in teams, each man handing the laths up to the next guy until they reach the top hangers who hang the four foot lath between two beams. Hangers are the stars. Especially the top guy strutting his stuff for eight hours, up under the shed roof shimmering in the summer sun.

But, I figure the hangers are the ones who could use some saltpeter. Hangers are mainly Puerto Ricans. This is a problem because some of the city kids have sisters under sixteen who had babies with Puerto Rican men. I tell you this stuff because back then, racism was a big part of our environment. It was everywhere. It defined us. As I state elsewhere in my story, if I was Black, I'd be pissed. And, I will never really know what it's like to be Black. I also doubt I'll ever know what's it like to be a hanger.

The Jamaicans always seem to have problems with us city boys. Jamaicans work hard. They drive tractors or doodlebugs (old stripped down Model A Fords). Jamaicans also drive us malingering city kids. I think they are afraid of losing their Green Card if they let up on us. "Git your sorry oss down dot row mon!"

Here I am sitting in the row waiting for the field boss to mark my arm with mercurochrome so I'll only pick leaves longer than 13 inches. Over the course of the summer we'll return to the same field six or seven times, picking two or three of the lowest leaves from each plant. I look forward to picking later in the season because the leaves are higher on the stalk. Instead of humping my ass down the row, I can walk on my knees (knee pads help). Later I only have to stoop to pick the leaves and then, best of all, walk as I pick. Sometimes it does pay to be short in life, but not often enough.

Picking is done in three man teams—two pickers and a dragger. Each picker picks both right and left rows and places a pad of leaves for the dragger. The dragger fills what looks like a narrow canvas laundry basket with the picked pads and drags them to trailers which bring them to the shed. We get paid piece work by how many feet of row we pick and drag. Connecticut minimum wage is 66 cents an hour and like most menial labor in this world, you have to really hump to make more than the hourly minimum wage.

The Morehouse Boys

The students from Morehouse College are the only guys at Cullman that are fast enough to make more working piece-time than the flat hourly rate. In the face of scarce stateside labor during WW1, Cullman and other tobacco farmers made arrangements with Morehouse College, an all-male Black college in Atlanta, Georgia, to send students to the farm for the summer to pick tobacco. The arrangement lasted well into the 1950s. In 1944 a precocious fifteen-year-old was accepted for early admission to Morehouse. That summer he was included in the group that went to Cullman farm. He travelled by train from Atlanta to Hartford, Connecticut, then on to the farm in Simsbury by bus. In Atlanta he sat in a segregated car. As far as I know, this arrangement was all he had ever experienced. In Washington, DC he boarded a train that had no segregated cars. It was his first experience with northern integration. Throughout that first summer he attended an integrated church, saw movies in integrated theaters, ate in integrated restaurants, and shopped in integrated stores. The members of the First Church of Christ in Simsbury embraced these earnest hard-working young men.

His letters back home glowed with exhilaration at what he experienced. On his return to Atlanta, he once more changed trains in Washington. This time the fifteen-year-old must have seen the segregated car quite differently. Martin Luther King Jr. returned to Cullman in 1947 but it was that summer in 1944 that awakened young Martin to the possibilities of a world free from Jim Crow. It would be a few more years before I ever heard his name or connected him with Cullman.

City Kids, Poisons, & Memories

We kids from the city made up the rest of the workforce. We were picked up by old school buses or surplus army trucks well before 6 AM. Working on tobacco, as we call it, is an intense experience. Besides the heat and the sore backsides and knees, our hands are soon black from a pasty mix of tobacco juice and dirt. We call it nicotine and are sure it's going to stunt our growth or make us impotent. But at that age, we think a lot of things will do this. Meanwhile, we are oblivious to the chemicals sprayed on the plants to kill tobacco worms and control a fungus called tobacco mosaic. The smell of tobacco is strong and lasting. It doesn't leave us until school starts. In a way it never leaves. One hot summer night driving up Interstate 91 in southern Massachusetts, the unexpected scent from a tobacco field in the valley below hurls me back to the shimmering heat, nicotine hands, and sore ass. Some kid is singing "A Thousand Miles Away." For a brief moment, I'm humping down that row, a thousand miles away.

Sooner or later just about every kid falls asleep in the bathtub and/or wakes up in the middle of the night, grabs a sandwich his mother made for tomorrow's lunch, goes to the pickup spot waiting in vain wondering why everyone else is late. Rainy days when we ride all the way to the farm only to be told to go home are the worst. The canvas covering the trucks often does not cover the entire front, so the rain whips through the open canvas at 50 MPH. The scary part comes when some idiot starts messing around with his food. This often escalates and sometimes gets racial. The fear and pain always just below the surface, ready to blow up at the slightest misunderstanding or misinterpretation between alien cultures.

All I want to do is get home and crawl back into bed. Of course this changes if the rain lets up. Stores are not yet open but along with the bread, the bread man has already dropped off donuts, little Frisbee Pies, Hostess Twinkies, all that good stuff. The milk man follows suit with his chocolate milk and whip cream canisters just waiting to be snatched.

Labor Agitator

One day the rain turns me into a smartass teenage labor agitator. It's sprinkling by the time the bus brings us to the farm. We can't go into the fields right away because we may spread the tobacco mosaic fungus and the damp leaves may be too wet to hang in the sheds. All morning the clouds roll in. The sun comes out. The clouds roll back in. It's now coming on 1pm. The sun is shining. The farm bigwigs huddle and say it's a go. About 60 of us shuffle to the buses to take us out to the fields.

I call out to the farm manager. "Excuse me Mr. Partika, are we getting paid for this morning?" Partika glances at his father who gives him a slight nod no. "No kid you'll get paid for picking tobacco this afternoon."

"But you kept us here all morning. The last time it rained and you kept us we got paid for the whole morning. Five hours. That's the law ain't it?"

Partika's sunburned face turns a slight shade redder. "Look you little…" Partika's father interrupts. "Listen son, we are giving you a chance to make some money this afternoon. It's 1:30 already so let's get back to work."

"But sir! The most we can work this afternoon is about three hours. If we don't work we get paid for five."

The elder Partika: "If that's what's bothering you we can keep working to make up the five hours."

"Yeah, but even if we did that it would be like working for nothing."

By now, guys are beginning to make some noise along the lines of "Fuck this! I ain't working till no moon comes up, man."

A tight little blink and "Alright boys! On the bus. The fields are still a bit wet anyway!" As I step on the bus, Partika looks up. "What's your name boy?"

It didn't rain the rest of the summer.

The Fastest White Boy On the Bus

We're starting a new row when I see that the team next to us is a Morehouse team. We don't see much of the Morehouse guys. They usually work in other fields and keep to themselves. The straw boss seldom misses an opportunity to remind us that they make more than we do because they work harder. Our piece-time numbers seldom approach the minimum wage rate. We envy the Morehouse Boys. To us, the Morehouse Boys are men.

I look back and see this Morehouse guy in the next row getting ready to pick. He's big with a gold front tooth. Without thinking I pick up my pace. He starts about 15 feet behind me in a 200 foot row. I hear his leaves snapping. I glance back. It looks like he's hardly moving but somehow he gains on me. I go into high gear. Gold Tooth moves closer but I'm not sure he knows he's in a race, not even sure he knows I exist. He looks calm, even relaxed. We're about half way to the end. I come to a section where the field goes a bit uphill. The ground is dryer. And I don't have to pick short withered leaves. I check the length of a leaf. Too small! I scramble forward about ten feet on my hands and knees and gain another five feet on Gold Tooth. Fifty feet to go. My shoulders ache. I'm humping so fast I almost run into the tent at the end of the row. I WON! Goddam! I won. I beat a Morehouse guy! As I pass him I give Gold Tooth a smirk. He smiles. When we walk out of the row Gold Tooth turns to me. "Hey man, what's your name."

"Jack"

He smiles again. "Well Jeeaack. Nice Pickin'."

A few days later, as we get off the bus, the straw boss yells out "Hey! Where's Jack." Then the bastard says, "You know, little Jack." Even though that pisses me off, I'm more afraid the Farm Manager is finally going to get even for my labor agitation last week. Instead the Straw Boss marches me over to the Morehouse truck and stands me in front of Gold Tooth.

"This the one?"

"He's the one."

"So Jack, Horace's picking partner got sick so Horace asked for you as a picking partner. What do you say?"

I say "Okay."

After the straw boss leaves, Horace turns to the Morehouse guys. "Hey listen up! My man Jeeaack says Okay. Treat him real good now cause ya'll owe him a morning's pay from last week.

He's our little lawyer."

Looking Back

The rest of the summer I pinch hit whenever the Morehouse Boys need a picker. They joke around and get silly, same as us, except they definitely work harder. They call me Little Jack or sometime Lawyer Jack, or even Sir Jackwick, whatever that's supposed to mean, but I don't mind. Don't mind at all. I am the fastest white boy on the bus.

I remember one day riding to another field in the Morehouse truck, Horace turned to me, "Hey Jeeaack, why you so serious?" The question took me by surprise. I gave him some weak wise-guy response. He just smiled. I had no clue about looking serious or not. That's not why I remember that brief exchange. What I remember was that a grown man paid me some attention. Looking back these sixty plus years, I realize that Horace could not have been much more than twenty but, to me, he was a man. A man who paid attention. He was a leader in his quiet confident way. So, here was a leader of men checking me out. I still remember that.

SHOE SHINE

The first job I almost had was shining shoes. I was about ten. I remember me and my buddy Skippy building our shoeshine kits. We spent a lot of time arguing about how to make the perfect shoe rack where the customer would rest his shoe so we could snap that rag, make those shoes sparkle, make our customers want to dance. We also spent a lot of money on brushes, buffing cloths, leather conditioner and especially shoe polish. Black, brown, tan, cordovan, even oxblood, all Kiwi brand! Nothing but the best!

It's finally Saturday morning. We carry our shoeshine kits downtown, walking instead of taking the bus because Skippy doesn't want to eat into the profits. We set up right outside G. Fox department store. That's nine stories of the richest people in Harford, all buying shoes and stuff. We figure at least half of them will want a good shoeshine after doing all that shopping. Skippy wants to set up on the entrance nearest the bus stop. We start to argue. I want to flip a coin. He says he called it first. I'm getting pretty mad when this tall kid with bad teeth walks up.

"Hey you two, waddya think you're doin'?"

"What does it look like we're doin'?"

"Takin my spot! That's what you're doin'."

"We got here first."

"First! My ass! I been here since Easter! Besides, you little jerks ain't got no license."

"Whaddya mean, license?"

Badteeth points to a blue metal tag with some numbers nailed to his shoeshine box, "You need a Street Vendor Class D Boot Black license dodo! You breakin' the law man! He looks to the sky and shrugs. I guess you'll enjoy reform school. But, … tell you what, you give me that there can of oxblood and run all the way home like good little boys and I won't tell no cop."

I reluctantly hand over the can of oxblood. But, Skippy is shaking his head no. Badteeth turns to Skippy. Before he can say anything, Skippy gets in his face, grabs the can of oxblood from his hand and says, "You want blood? I'll give you blood! And, it won't be no shoe polish. Asshole!"

Badteeth just shrugs, tap his license plate and smiles. Badteeth walks over to a doorman who actually does have a pretty cool looking uniform. Badteeth points at us.

It's a long walk home. When we get back to the project, Skippy walks up the hill right into Leroy's Grooming Emporium and guess what? He gets a job.

He's the only white kid I ever knew who was a shoeshine boy in a black barber shop. When he grew up, I heard he made a whole pile of money. I can tell you he surely did hate to part with money, I bet he still has that can of oxblood stuffed deep in some drawer alongside a stack of valuable baseball cards.

A New Bike

"Hey Jackie, your father went downtown."

"So?"

There was a hint of a smirk in Butchie's nasty little laugh. "He went on your bike!"

"What?" I looked in the yard. It was gone. "When?"

"I dunno, about two hours ago."

Damn! This was my new bike, my first store-bought bike—a Schwinn. My mother worked so hard for it. Four dollars a day cleaning other people's houses. She took a lot of crap from Marholin's Department Store just to get the bike on credit. I started running downtown.

I know. My mother spoiled me buying a brand new bike but, she saw it as a life or death deal. I already had a bike. That was the problem. It was a bike I made. I stole the frame from the junkyard. Every time I got a little money I would head downtown to the Western Auto store and buy wheels, tires and tubes, a handlebar, the chain. I loved those chains—blue steel bathed in light oil. I can still feel the squirmy heft and smell that oil. It made me feel like I knew what I was doing, Next came the accessories—headlights, horns, fenders. Brakes were in the accessory category. That's what made my mother nervous.

At least I already got one legendary ride on the new bike. It was a hot Monday in July and Butchie had a great idea to ride to a carnival in Wilson about four miles up Rt. 5 from Hartford. I was dying to really put some miles on my new bike. Eight miles round trip and a carnival thrown in sounded good to me. I had a buck and a half and Butchie had about the same. When we got to the carnival it was being loaded onto huge trucks for the next carnival somewhere. We were crushed but we were also young, resilient, and optimistic which is another way of saying we were dumb-ass stupid. Now Butchie had his second big idea of the day. "So let's go to Riverside Park instead." Riverside Park (now known as Six Flags New England) was in Agawam, Massachusetts twenty-six miles away. "What the hell! We already got four miles in. Being only ten I let Butchie do the math. Well we pedaled and pedaled. We pedaled those fat heavy balloon tire bikes. Back then we thought the so-called English racer bikes were for English people and other foreigners prone to sandals and short pants.

Fortunately Rt. 5 back then went through farm country. Coming from the city we assumed all farmers were dumb. We stopped at farm houses and, without asking, drunk directly from hoses or outside spigots. Sometimes we would get yelled at but that was nothing new. Adults were the enemy even when they're nothing but dumb hicks.

I am proud to say that we made all twenty-six miles to Riverside Park that day and luck was with us. Riverside Park was closed on Mondays. We stood there in the parking lot watching this stupid mechanical clown rocking back and forth laughing a hideous monotonous laugh from inside this hideous glass booth. Somehow the glass booth brought to mind an earlier carnival where for fifteen cents you could go into a tent and look at a paralyzed polio kid staring at you from a mirror atop his iron lung. I wanted to throw a brick through that glass clown booth. I wanted to stop this brainless clown sonofabitch from laughing at us— laughing a never-ending hollow laugh. I say luck was with us because it took all our money, all of our time, and more than all of our energy to pedal those bikes back home. We split a foot-long hotdog with the works and a large Coke with our last 75 cents. It was heaven. It got us through. I would strongly recommend it to Lance Armstrong. We got back in the dark, our mothers were frantic. I marvel at it still. Today we would already have our pictures on milk cartons. We never told our mothers of our plans because there were none.

But now I had to plan. Should I start at his favorite tavern? What if he already sold my bike? Could I buy it back if he sold it on the cheap? If not, should I find a cop? Would Dad get arrested? I was almost at the Tunnel, a big intersection in Hartford that's the boundary between downtown and the Black section I had just run through. I saw him wobbling through the intersection, knees almost hitting his chin. I ran into the street. I thought he was going to run over me. Then he saw me and broke into his famous shit-eating grin. "Ya didn't think I was gonna sell it did ya?"

"Give me the bike, dad."

PAPER DRIVE

When I was about seven years old, our St. Michael parish, along with many other parishes of the time, had a paper drive. You could sell old newspapers by the pound. Schools, at least the Catholic schools, had us kids bring old newspaper to school. People would stack newspaper out on their tenement porches or in their garages where we would collect them.

The Granger family lived in the unit behind ours in the Nelton Court project. The youngest boy was a year or so older than me. Two older brothers were what I would consider "Big Kids." I don't remember much about their mother and in my memory, the boys are now just a weak blur of straw-like hair and crooked teeth.

I do remember the father a little better. There weren't a lot of men in the project at the time so his mustache stood out for me. The mustache was tightly trimmed leaving a thin line originating from just below each nostril heading a short ways downward then each making a neat 90 degree turn away from the philtrum leaving just enough room above the upper lip for a sweet wet kiss. In other words, it was just like Clark Gable's mustache, and like Clark Gable, Mr. Granger also had big ears, but that is clearly where any resemblance with Clark ends. It was pretty obvious that his boys got the straw hair and all from their father.

The main reason I remember any of this family is because I was introduced to a world of bunking school and stealing other folks' old newspapers. I can't remember how I got in their charge. Most likely, my mother made a deal with the now forgettable Mrs. Granger to watch me and send me off to school while my mother caught an early bus out to the suburbs to get an early start cleaning other people's houses.

Whatever, I had the good luck of ending up in Mr. Granger's care on the day he decided his sons were going to delay their academic education to learn a few things about self-reliance, opportunism, and filching old newspaper from churches. Mr. Granger drove us out of our parish (St.

Michael's) to a new parish (St. Justin's) where old newspaper openly flourished, most of it tied in neat bundle's that seemed to cry out "Take me! Take me! I'm a neat little package!" Obviously Mr. Granger had planned this carefully. He knew just where the good stuff was. He had a grid worked out in his head. He dropped each son at a pickup spot informing each, of their expected pickup time. He also provided each son with rosary beads and a scapular to be hung around the neck.

"Hey Jacky, if anyone gives you any shit, tell them Father O'Brien, the St. Michaels Pastor told us that Father Nolan at St. Justin's said we are all children of God and all God's children should share our bounty."

I was too small to carry bundles of newspaper, even the neat ones. And maybe Mr. Granger was aware of the penalties for contributing to the delinquency of a minor. At any rate, I got to ride around with him in his old beater station wagon that had real wood panels on the side doors. The car even had a radio which Mr. Granger played all day long. Mostly big band and crooner stuff. He took time out to listen to Stella Dallas. I thought he was going to cry a few times. I loved it all! A radio in a car! Music and stories. What next?

It was a real productive day. We could hardly fit in the car and had to lay on top of all those papers. We must have made a fortune. But, Mr. Granger never told me. He gave me a scapular and told me to tell my mother I got it at school that day.

EASTER LILIES

Folks who do bad things ain't always bad, and folks who do good things surely ain't always good.

Back when I was nine or ten, we kids loved Saturdays. Saturday was downtown day. After walking the mile or so our first stop was Hartford's Strand Theater. It promised two feature films, a couple of serials like *The Mask of Zorro* and *Red Rider with Little Beaver*. I always wanted to be Little Beaver. I especially loved his cool feather. We also got the news from 20th Century Fox Movietone News and, best of all, 50 cartoons. We never got all they promised, but the promise was too good to ignore, too good to question. We bought packages of Jujubes to throw at the screen and each other. Movie ushers hated us.

Next came the department stores, G. Fox and Brown Thompson became our playground. We competed with each other to pinch the most expensive or outrageous item. The ten story G. Fox was the classiest department store in Hartford. It had a whole wall of elevators manned by men in real classy uniforms. Besides being Little Beaver, I wanted to be an elevator man, but all the elevator men were Black so I figured I couldn't make the cut. The G. Fox floor walkers were dressed in dapper suits and ties. Maintaining that classy aura took priority over chasing after dirty little street urchins and we took full advantage. Brown Thompson (second classiest store) paid a bit more attention to us but let us experiment on one of those X-ray machines where you could see the bones in your feet right through your shoes. It evoked considerable scientific curiosity as we stuck a variety of body parts and objects where our feet should have been. I still await the prospect of foot and toe cancer.

We also stopped at the five & ten chain stores, W. T. Grant, Woolworths, and S. S. Kresge's. The floorwalkers there were far more interested in our shenanigans than in maintaining decorum. They would even run after us, no class at all! They knew what we were up to. We did get a little painted turtle once but could never nail one of the goldfish that were sold in little plastic bags. Jackknives were lusted after but were kept in a locked glass case.

Finally, we would make it to the Wadsworth Atheneum for some real adventure. The Atheneum was packed throughout with mummies, knights in armor, guns, and model boats, all kinds of neat stuff. It also had world class paintings and sculptures, but we paid them no attention except for some of the nudes. No, we were there for adventure. It seemed to us that you had to be over one hundred years old to get a job on the Atheneum security staff. We were quick. These guys lurched along almost as slow as the mummies they watched over. Years later my seventy-year-old uncle Jim Griffin got a job at the Atheneum. Messing around in the Atheneum wasn't so much fun anymore.

One Saturday afternoon, I didn't have the carfare to take the bus back home. I walked up North Main Street alone. I had to go past a cemetery, the city jail, and through the Black part of town. There was a grocery store up ahead that had all kinds of fruit, vegetables, and flowers displayed out on the sidewalk. The storeman had started putting things back inside. Just as I was passing the store, a large lady came along with an even larger dog. Storeman didn't look too happy. I think he knew large lady and knew her dog even better. He turned and picked up an empty peach basket and headed for the dog. The dog was doing a lot of sniffing and didn't seem to notice the shopkeeper heading at him. That's when big dog lifted his leg and watered some collards.

Storeman started running at the dog. Large Lady screamed that the big dog she called Mr. Bow Wow would tear Storeman a new asshole if he messed with her or Mr. Bow Wow. She yanked hard on Mr. Bow Wow's leash. Mr. Bow Wow growled and pulled at the leash. I heard a police siren coming closer but didn't know if the cops were coming here or to some other killing. It began to dawn on me that no one was paying me any attention, so I just picked up the flower pot and started slowly walking away. If the shopkeeper saw me, I planned to start crying because I was scared of dogs and grownups fighting. I never had to execute the plan. The toughest part was carrying that heavy pot for about a mile and hold it in a way that the big white blossoms didn't fall off. When I got home I remembered tomorrow was Easter and my new flowers were Easter Lilies. I hid the plant in the closet and after mom went to bed, I put it on the table. When I got up the next morning, my mother was already up and asked, "Where did that come from"

"Downtown."

"Did it cost much?"

"Not much."

"What are you going to do with them?"

"Oh! They're for you Mom."

She turned away. She didn't want me to see her tears. For the next fifty years I gave her an Easter Lily every Easter morning. I didn't even mind paying for them.

5

CRIME & PUNISHMENT

CUBAN HEELS

It was getting dark and beginning to rain a hard October rain when my buddy Rumpy Raposa told me my mother was looking for me. This seemed strange because I seldom missed supper and the rain was getting nastier. As I approached my unit, I could see a police car's flashing lights; the cop was in my kitchen. I knew the jig was up. I thought about running away but it was too close to supper. As I entered the house my mother started crying and screaming at me.

That was the worst. I always figured things out for myself. With all my youthful adventures and misadventures, my mother never hit me and I never wanted to hurt her. Right now, I just wanted to cry. The cop actually helped me and my mother out. "We're just gonna take your son downtown for a while Mrs. Barry. He should be home tonight." It was a long drive downtown.

When we get to the police station, the cop brings me to a basement room where my best friend Joe Kelly and Joe's year younger twin brothers Tom and Mickey are sitting on folding chairs around a beat-up metal desk. A uniformed cop and a detective named Deegan are trying to look pissed. Deegan has been reassigned to Juvenile after pleading nolo to a Domestic Assault and got sent down to Juvenile until his case gets cleared. Deegan even looks like a Deegan. He's sitting on the desk cleaning an enormous forty-five pistol with a dirty handkerchief. Without a word or even a look, he directs me to pull up a chair. As soon I sit down my so called best friend Joe puts his hand on my arm like he's some kind of priest and says "Tell them Jack. They know everything." What the fuck! ... I mean we made a vow to never squeal. Some vow! I decide to stick with the no squeal vow just to show Joe that I'm not a rat. I look at Joe. I try to look shocked.

"What!... Joe said that?"

Deegan jumps off the desktop and shoves the forty-five under my nose.

"What! What! What! Don't give me that shit!"

"Mickey here says he gave you Jack, you Joe, you Tommy and some badass named Henry Kovnowski most of the $1,000 money order money he robbed from Ozzies drugstore. "Where the fuck is that money? Where is this Henry fuck!" Deegan's approach to interrogation by screaming four letter words and wielding a big ass gun at us sounded good, but the only money Deegan got that night was 300 bucks I was hiding for Mickey. All the rest of the stolen money was long gone. Man! How did I get into this mess? Deegan is impatient, he slaps me on the back. "So Jack let's go get that money you hid."

Deegan wore a suit and pointy tan dress shoes. He's evidently unaware of the fact that a lot of Connecticut is covered with red clay and unaware it's raining. I had made sure I buried the money where people (even kids) were not likely to go. We are heading up a steep bank right into the heart of an abandon brickyard. The uniformed cop trips on a root, slips in the clay and knocks Deegan off his feet. They both come up looking like statues, red statues, pissed off statues. Deegan's tan shoes are red and squishy. I'm okay. I think they want to kill me! I know I better come up with that money jar. And, I do!

As far as the robbery goes, I swear! I had nothing to do with it. The Kelly boys were strapping, blond hair, blue eyed kids, but for anyone who knew them, it was clear they were crazy as hell. Ozzie hired Mickey when he was about thirteen. He had a pinball machine at the rear of the store where kids hung out. At some point Mickey noticed a lot of money in the cigar box where all Money Order business was kept. One day when Ozzie stepped out, Mickey took the cash in the cigar box behind the counter and buried it behind Ozzie's store. Everybody knew he took it, but for months, Mickey wouldn't crack. Part of the legend has it that the FBI got involved because stealing money orders was a federal offense. This didn't faze Mickey. He even gave testimony about seeing a strange man in the store that morning. When asked for a description he said the man was Black and had one brown eye and one blue. One of the legends among the kids was that Mickey forgot where in Ozzy's back yard he buried the money. And he got Henry Kovonowski to figure out exactly where it was. I never found out why Mickey decided to confess after outwaiting the law for months but I did say he was crazy didn't I.

Deegan came back and bullied us occasionally during those months trying to find out where all that money went. He was wasting his time. All the kids knew where it went. They went horseback riding in Keney Park in Hartford until they got kicked out for trashing the golf course by running horses over the putting greens. I would have none of it, but not for any moral consideration. It had more to do with my fear and dislike of those fat dumb-ass Keney Park horses. They would rather eat grass than take me where I wanted to go.

Anyway, I finally got very involved one night when Joe, Mickey, and I were watching TV while their mother was cooking supper a few short feet away in the kitchen. Mickey started to talk about a book he was reading. He said he thought I would like it. I was surprised that he could read. It didn't matter. He started rifling through the book. Holy Cow! It seemed there was a twenty on every damn page. I grabbed the book. You may think this is all bullshit but I grabbed that book purely on a reflex to protect Mickey and in a way, protect his mother who proclaimed his innocence long and loud all along. But, it didn't take me long after I hid the money to start thinking about that electric guitar I always wanted. Hey Bo Diddley, step back!

Finally the phone rang. They got Henry! Deegan pulled out the dirty handkerchief and started cleaning dried red clay off his shoes. a long half hour later, the yard gate opened, headlights swept through the rain. We heard the click click click of Henry's Cuban Heels through the narrow basement window.

When Henry finally walked into that room It seemed like he barely came up to the doorknob. Deegan, who was sitting on a radiator trying to dry off, put his head in his hands. I thought he was going to be sick or something. But he started to laugh. He laughed and laughed. Then, we all laughed too.

SNOW GOOSE BOOK REPORT

Young people often create their own value system. They become what is commonly referred to as "teenagers." But whatever was at play back then, most of us did go to school. Our report cards reflected a more innocent 1950s version of Ghetto upside-downness. A perfect report card for us was:

1. exactly 180 days of attendance—the state minimum required attendance to pass;
2. the lowest citizenship grade possible;
3. straight "Ds" or whatever minimum it took to graduate on-time and get on with our real lives.

It was frosting on the cake when the report would also tell us how smart we were "if we only applied ourselves."

I came damn close to not making it out on time. In my senior year I had to pass both Senior and Sophomore English and even needed the quarter credit from Mr. Selza, the much despised gym teacher, to make the 16 credit minimum.

There were a number of reasons I flunked Sophomore English while sailing through Junior English. But, *Kon-Tiki* had a lot to do with it. It was another damn book report thing. Mrs. McQueeny knew I had finally signed out *Kon-Tiki* from the school library only three days before the book report was due on Friday. By the time I got home on Wednesday, I was running a 104 degree temp with a wicked sore throat. Despite burning eyes, I started to read that book. I read, slept, drifted. For three long days I was on that raft, burning in the tropics, cooled by the Pacific breeze and splashed by those crazy fish jumping onto the raft. I turned in my book report on time on Friday.

Mrs. McQueeney didn't believe me. Didn't believe I could read that book and write a report in three days. She said "I read that book in college. It took me a lot longer than three days, young man!" That started a long, slow, inevitable slide that resulted in me having to take Sophomore English twice. I'm not complaining. It was somewhat comforting to be victim of such absolute evil. I mean, have you ever had to read *A Tale of Two Cities* exactly ten pages per week, no more, no less, twice in one childhood? I did for flunking Sophomore English twice. It truly was the worst of times.

So, what does all this have to do with *Snow Goose?* During my second tour of Sophomore English I had to pick from a list of about fifty books and do a book report. That's where I found *Snow Goose. Kon-Tiki* surely made me leery of book reports but, I loved *Snow Goose!* I really did. It's a novella by Paul Gallico first published in 1940 in *The Saturday Evening Post,* then expanded to a book. I don't have a copy of my original book report. If Wikipedia existed in 1959, the following would have been my book report:

The "Snow Goose" is set against a backdrop of war and "The Miracle of Dunkirk" where more than 340,000 Allied soldiers were saved from the German Army when a hastily assembled flotilla of over 800 boats including civilian pleasure and fishing boats carried them from France back to England.

This story is a parable of the regenerative power of friendship and love. It documents the growth of a friendship between a disabled artist living in an abandoned lighthouse in Dunkirk, and a local girl who finds a wounded snow goose and brings it to the artist. Their friendship blossoms as they nurse the snow goose back to health. The bird revisits the lighthouse in its seasonal migration for several years. Having saved hundreds of soldiers in the retreat from Dunkirk, the artist, his small sailboat and the snow goose, disappear. The bird returns briefly to the now grown girl. She interprets this as the artist's soul taking farewell of her and realizes she had come to love him. Afterwards, a German pilot destroys the lighthouse along with all of the artist's work, except for one portrait the girl saves. It is a painting of her as the artist first saw her, a child, with the wounded snow goose in her arms.

As I said earlier, I really liked this book and feel fortunate to have found it. I read it eagerly and couldn't wait to tell my buddies in Sophomore English. The entire book was only 57 pages, big print and even had some drawings. My buddies were most appreciative.

SIX SHOOTER

Ned Cosgrove was a good friend of mine. Although he lived a couple of miles away from the project, we went to the same grammar school and high school. More important we went to the same two year technical school after high school. It was important because Ned had a car and I didn't. I got lucky. If he didn't go to that school I never would have gone. I didn't even know how to drive a car.

Now Ned's car wasn't much of a car. It was a 14-year-old Chevy coupe that might have once been blue but was now a faded primer-coat gray freckled with rust. But, as sad as this car was, it could be said that it changed my life by giving me that chance to further my education. Ned's mother and father were really nice people even though Ned's father was a cop. I think both his parents liked me and were glad to help me out. I know I was sure glad.

One warm summer afternoon in 1960 the car came damn close to changing my life once again, but I got lucky. We got lucky. "We," in this case, were me, Ned, and my two-year-old nephew, Bobby. I was watching him for my sister. We were sitting on the stoop of my home in the project. It was across the street from a row of four-story yellow brick apartment houses. One of the apartments was used as an unlicensed beauty parlor. I don't remember what we were doing or thinking because whatever it was got blown away by the BAM! BAM! BAM! of gunshots, followed by a brief moment of utter silence, then a wail I'll never forget. "SHE'S DEAD! SHE'S DEAD! SHE'S DEAD!" Ned looked at me and announced, "Hey! Those were gunshots!"

I added, "And it ain't from a twenty-two either!"

In the short time that we're stuck between curiosity and fear, a tall Black man runs out of the apartment across the street, tucks a large pistol in his waistband, and sprints up the hill to his car. By now, a full chorus of shrieks from the apartment fills the street. The gunman pulls out onto the street. His car nudges a faded grayish car parked in front of him. That's right. He nudges the bumper of Ned's old Chevy coupe beater, then starts down the street.

I don't know if it's in the gene pool of cop's kids or if at that moment in time Ned is nuttier than the gunman. A gunman who had just grabbed his wife by the arm and blows her brains out in front of their twelve-year-old daughter. Ned runs the thirty feet to the curb, points his finger at the man in the car and shouts, "STOP! YOU HIT MY CAR!" Ned sounds just like a cop. The car slows to a stop. The man looks at Ned through the open window and gives him a long thoughtful look.

At that moment it occurs to me that we are no longer the audience. We're in the movie—it was like someone hit the pause button. I couldn't move, afraid any sudden movement would restart the action. Afraid Ned's going to get shot and die right in front of me. What'll I tell his mom and dad? I'm afraid one forty-five slug will go right through me and hit little Bobby. What'll my sister do? I'm afraid I'm going to die!

The car starts down the hill slowly picking up speed. Ned hurries back to the stoop.

"NED! What the hell were you thinking?"

"Waddya mean?"

"You could have gotten killed—got us all killed!"

Ned pauses. "No way!"

"Why the hell not?"

"Because he didn't have any bullets left in his gun."

"And how would you know that?"

Ned patiently stretches out each word. "Because … I … counted … six … shots."

Ned never lived that "only six shots bullshit down." But, he did make some amends though. His father the cop would be proud. After being ignored by the cops, Ned went next door and phoned in the make and license number of the car. It turns out the gunman was an ex-Marine, Korean War veteran who suffered from what we now call PTSD. He drove home, and shot himself in the stomach. The cops got there in time to get him to the hospital. You might say Ned saved the man's life, or whatever was left of it.

We never did find the spot on the bumper that got nudged, and the beater continued to help get us get educated until about a year later when a priest ran a stop sign and totaled Ned's car with me riding shotgun. The priest had a hard time convincing the cops that he, the priest was at fault.

SIXTY-SEVEN MINUTES OF JUSTICE

(**Author's note:** *I was born in the same year, 1941, as Emmitt Till.*)

I was born July 25, 1941 in Chicago, the year they bombed Pearl Harbor and started the big war. My daddy Louis joined the army and ended up in Italy—dead. They tell me he was executed for something they call willful misconduct. I don't know. I ain't never even seen him. I was an only child and my Mama Mamie loved me. That I do remember. She was an amazing woman alright. She was smart! She was the first Black kid to make the honor roll at a mostly white high school in Chicago. She called me Bobo. That's what everyone in the neighborhood called me.

I liked my neighborhood. Back then folks were making good money over in the factories and stock yards. We had a lot of nice stores and businesses all over the South Side. My Mama was a hard worker too. Worked twelve hours a day. I helped out with the cleaning, cooking, and laundry at home even though I was just getting over Polio. But I was happy. Had lots of friends in school. Liked to make folks laugh. My buddy Richard used to say I had a suitcase full of laughs.

Man! That suitcase sure is empty now. I still can't believe it. In August 1955, when I was fourteen, Uncle Mose came up from Mississippi to take my cousin Wheeler back South to visit relatives. When I heard about this, I begged Mama to let me go too. She did not like this idea at all. Instead she wanted to visit relatives in Omaha, Nebraska with me, but she finally said okay. She even gave me my daddy's ring engraved with his initials "LT." I was so excited the next day at the 63rd Street Station kissing Mama goodbye and getting on that southbound train with Uncle

Mose and Wheeler. When we got to Money, Mississippi I was so glad I talked Mama into letting me go.

I really liked my cousins. But, except for picking cotton, there wasn't much going on in Money, so my suitcase was jam packed full of laughs. I had them all laughing—even the older cats. After a few days of picking cotton, we went to Bryant's Grocery and Meat Market to buy some soda pop and candy. I remember thinking we had a thousand stores in Chicago better than this rusty-dusty little place. I do remember wanting this white lady running the store to know that I was from Chicago. Wanted to show the Money boys how black folks in Chicago ain't scared of no whites. I remember smiling my big smile and saying goodbye.

To tell you the truth, I don't remember much else. No big thing, you know? That's why I couldn't figure out what was happening when Roy Bryant, the store owner and his half-brother J.W. Milam came pounding on Uncle Mose's door in the middle of the night looking for the smart mouthed kid from Chicago. As bad as it was for me, I will always grieve what it done to Uncle Mose. And I give him so much credit for later, standing up in that courtroom, pointing his finger at Mr. Bryant and saying, "Dar he!" It's a wonder he was not killed. As for me, I can't remember much and I'm glad of it. I'm told I was brutally beaten, shot in the head, tied with barbed wire to a big metal fan, and thrown into the Tallahatchie River. Man! These cats were good at being bad. I mean real bad!

Did you ever look at a picture of you dead? I don't recommend it. I looked so bad, the only way they knew it was me was I still had my Daddy's "LT" ring on. It really bothered me when Mama made them keep my casket open for five long days before the funeral back in Chicago. More than 100,000 people saw my body lying in that casket. And, when that picture of me was put in *Jet Magazine* and the *Chicago Defender*, even white folk got disgusted.

This was good, but not good enough. As bad as all this stuff was, it got way worse. On September 23 1955, the jury of all white all men found Mr. Bryant and Mr. Milam NOT GUILTY of all charges. It took them folks all of 67 minutes to figure that out. But that ain't the worst of it. A few months later, Mr. Bryant and Mr. Milam sold the whole story of how they kidnapped and killed me to *Look* magazine for $4,000. No one could touch them because of double jeopardy.

One hundred days after my murder, Rosa Parks refused to give up her seat on an Alabama city bus. She said "I thought about Emmett Till, and I just couldn't go back to the back of the bus." Nine years later, Congress passed the Civil Rights Act of 1964. We say things are better now. But I heard where a bus load of college educated kids in Mississippi were riding down the highway yelling stuff about hanging Blacks. Now, even our own president says bad stuff! We still say, we have a long way to go. Yes sir! We still do!

BACHELOR YEARS

6

War & Peace

As I mentioned in the Forward I was born in Hartford, Connecticut. Born on what was then Armistice Day, November 11, 1941 and baptized on December 7, 1941, the day Pearl Harbor was attacked. I was named John Barry after my father. John Barry also happened to be the name of the so-called father of the American Navy. Later, in the Army, I often pondered that militaristic beginning, for, just as with so many young men going off to serve their country, I was no warrior, I was also no lover, much to my despair at the time.

Even though I had graduated from a two-year technical school majoring in electronics, I was unable to get a real job because of my A-1 draft status, which at the time meant no one was willing to hire me. Hence, I volunteered for the draft in 1962. Volunteering for the draft required two years of service instead of three for enlisting. This was during that brief interlude between the Korean "Police Action" and the Vietnam War. While my time in the "peacetime" Army did include standard military episodes of intense boredom, frantic lunacy, and utter confusion, it did not compare in any way to real combat. I never faced what so many of my brothers faced. I believe if I were drafted one or two years later I would have joined real soldiers, fighting in Vietnam. I would have joined them not because I was patriotic or thought the Domino Theory made any sense. Right or wrong, I would have ended up over there because I needed a job, because I couldn't afford to hide in college, and because I thought I was smarter than the Army and I would never die.

WARNING! In my army, the "F" word wasn't much more than a glottal tic. There may be some folk who have the skills to write about the army without using profanity. I am not one of them. As Patton explained: "It may not sound nice to some bunch of little old ladies at an afternoon tea party, but it helps my soldiers to remember. You can't run an army without profanity; and it has to be eloquent profanity." Well la-di-fuckin'-da.

An Existential Lesson

She crossed the street coming right at me. Long loping cowboy strides. I didn't want to star - not cool - so I went back to my book. I was sitting in a little pocket park in downtown Lawton (as downtown as Lawton gets). I was in Oklahoma, along with 80,000 or so young men at Fort Sill, training to fire artillery shells (including "tactical" nuclear war heads) at our Soviet Cold War enemy who, as it turned out was stumbling into obscurity.

It was the morning after payday, the day the eagle shits. After what seemed like a lifetime of confinement, payday would unleash a monthly carnival of testosterone-fueled frustration in many forms including sex, homesickness, and inarticulate violence—all nourishing the Lawton economy. Throw more sawdust on the barroom floor, hose the broken bottles and vomit off the street, turn up the amp, and get ready for another good payday night.

But, no Friday night cleavage and empty smile for me! No Sir! I was no sucker. Besides I didn't have money for the 3.2% Oklahoma Bible Belt beer. Most of all I couldn't stand the noise. I was a dud flirting at 140 decibels. I grew to avoid Diana Ross. By now, our national fear of the possibility of an occasional silence at gatherings has me looking forward to funerals and dreading weddings. Especially weddings taken over by DJs.

So, it was the quiet of a Saturday morning in the park, not the deafening pantomime courtship of Friday night for me. And, I could wear my own 1960s East Coast Intellectual uniform: trench coat, grubby khakis, low cut scruffy sneakers, a pipe, and a serious book.

"HOW YA DOIN'?"

As they say in Oklahoma, she looked rode hard and put back wet. She was flat chest skinny, a bright smile hiding behind missing teeth.

Looked to be in her thirties but could have been a lot younger. She had matted brown hair, tight jeans, and red cowboy boots with Cuban heels. Maybe that's why she walked like a man. She looked tough enough but it was her jumpy energy that struck me—scared me in a way. Like a puppy off its leash running in traffic, unpredictable, vulnerable. And, she was in my space.

"SO, HOW YAWL DOIN'?"

"Uh, ok I guess"

"I GUESS? ... DONCHA KNOW?"

"Yeah. Sure!"

"SO, HOW YA DOIN'?"

This was the first woman I had talked to in at least a month and so far it wasn't going so well.

"I'm fine. Uh, how about you?"

"OH! I'M FINE TOO. JUST FINE, FINE, FINE! YOU A SOLDIER?"

"Yeah."

"I LIKE SOLDIER BOYS! YOU GOT ANY MONEY?"

"No."

"SHEEEIT! C'MON! I KNOW YOU GOT SOME MONEY!"

"Nope! I only get $22.50 a month. The rest of my pay goes home to my mother. Got just enough for a coffee and the bus back to post."

"WELL, YOU A GOOD SON ANYWAY. HOW OLD ARE YOU?"

"Twenty one" I lied.

"LOOK AWFUL YOUNG TO BE SMOKIN A PIPE! MY DADDY SMOKED A PIPE. HE'S DEAD NOW. LUNGS! YOU A PROFESSOR OR SUMTHIN'?"

A nervous laugh. "No!"

"WHAT YOU READIN?"

I held up the book.

"*THE FALL*! WHO WROTE THAT?"

"Albert Kamuss."

Being a self-taught East Coast Intellectual, M. Camus sounded Kamoo to me. I also was into Jeen Paul Sartray and Andrew Guide. I understood Camus about as well as I pronounced his name, but, found a kind of comfort in the rhythm of those nobly depressing words neatly laid out on the printed page. But right now comfort was long gone.

"MAN! I KNOW ABOUT FALLS! HELL, I EVEN TOOK A FALL LAST NIGHT! DIDN'T GET OUT TILL THIS MORNING. CAN'T WAIT TO GET BACK TO DALLAS. THEY WORK ON REAL SHIT DOWN THERE. DON'T GO MESSIN' WITH PEOPLE JUST HAVIN' A LITTLE FUN. KNOW WHAT I MEAN?"

"You were in jail?"

"I JUST TOLE YA DIDN'T I? JUST GOT OUT! ONE HUNDRED BUCKS OR THREE DAYS. HAD TO WAIT FOR THE BAIL MAN TO OPEN. MISSED MY RIDE BACK TO DALLAS. NOW I HAVE TO WAIT FOR SOMEONE TO COME ALL THE WAY BACK UP HERE TO COLLECT ME AND BRING MY SORRY ASS BACK TO DALLAS!

"But..."

"MISSED MY RIDE BECAUSE OF THAT LITTLE SHIT JUDGE! I WOULDN'T PISS IN THAT MOTHERFUCKER'S MOUTH IF HIS BELLY WAS ON FIRE! SWEAR TO GOD, A COLD GLASS OF WATER AND A GOOD PIECE OF ASS WOULD LIKELY KILL HIM.

"Yeah but..."

"COULD OF TAKEN THE BUS BACK TO DALLAS IF HE DIDN'T TAP ME OUT. YOU REALLY GOT NO MONEY?"

"No. Sorry." And I was.

"SHEEEIT! WELL NICE TALKIN' TO YA ANYWAYS"

And with that she loped across the street and around a corner. My pipe was out. I put it in my pocket.

OK CITY

After months of unjust delay, I finally got a weekend pass and a chance to get off post. It's Saturday and it takes a while to get my first ride.

"Where ya headed?"

"Oklahoma City."

"I can only take ya to the next wah."

What the hell is a wah? Damn! This is gonna take me all weekend. As it turns out, a Y is where a road splits and the next Y for me is forty miles closer to Oklahoma City. As we pull out I notice there's a half pint bottle of Wild Turkey in the cupholder. The driver takes the bottle and, one handed, deftly half fills a Dixie cup propped between his legs and offers me a drink. It's still morning and besides I don't see another cup handy so I say "no thanks" but I do believe I'm going to like Oklahoma City after all.

So here I am after half a day of hitchhiking, sitting on a bench in a little park in downtown Oklahoma City under the blank-eyed statue gaze of Wiley Post. Wiley was a famous 1930s barnstorming Native American pilot who, as the plaque says, flew into eternity (really a lagoon in Alaska) along with his good friend humorist Will Rogers. I'm sure the patch over one of Wiley's eyes didn't help his perception much.

A few benches away a guy is killing a bottle in a paper bag. Welcome to the Bible Belt. I casually pat my pockets—big twenties in the right; ones in the left. I figure sooner or later he's going to hit me up for some money and I don't want to flash all my stash. Sure enough! He takes a deep breath sort of storing up the hot air that's coming and shuffles over.

"Excuse me, sir."

Sir? I'm a skinny twenty-year-old kid with a bad GI haircut. Who does he think he's fooling?

"Excuse me, sir. My name is Max Biermann. I'm trying to get back home to Ponca City. I got a job waiting tables. Could you please help me out?" Here I am with hardly any money not knowing where I'll sleep tonight and thirsty for something stronger than that 3.2% Bible Belt beer. So I say to Max, "No, but tell you what Max, I'll go a couple of bucks and we share the next bottle. Ok?"

While we're knocking off the bottle of sweet cheap wine in the park, I learn that Max just got out of the city jail that morning. In OK City back then public vagrancy gets you five days or five dollars. In 1972 the Supreme Court found such laws to be too vague. That was too late to help Max but a cell mate named Smiley did help him. Max got out after four days because Smiley passed the hat somehow and got the last dollar Max needed to get released early. There are no Sunday releases so

Max would not have gotten out until Monday. Max learns that I'm on a weekend pass from Fort Sill, don't much like the Army, have no room for the night yet, and my father is a drunk.

We make a plan. Max will wire his boss for twenty five bucks on the promise he'll show up for work Monday morning. When the money comes Max will use three bucks to bail Smiley out of the can and the three of us will rent a room, knock back a few and have a good old time. So, down to the Western Union office to send the telegram off to Ponca City. That done, we buy another bottle to shorten the wait. The wine is beginning to take its toll but we stick to the plan, and after a blurry couple of hours, we head back to the Western Union office.

Max smiles this crooked smile where you can't tell if he just remembered a good joke or just has to piss. He bellows "Howdy Little Lady!" The girl behind the Western Union counter reminds me of that American Gothic painting only younger and without the pitchfork; but every bit as severe, right down to the painful looking part in the middle of her head. Her nose keeps twitching. I think she's afraid she might get drunk on our fumes. "I mean morning Ma'am" *(It's late afternoon).* "You got some money for Max Bierman?" She slowly opens a drawer on the other side of the counter like she's expecting snakes to leap out and slither up her pale arms. She takes her time studying the one piece of paper in the drawer. Without answering Max's question she keeps her eyes on the piece of paper and asks "Do you have any identification… sir?" Max looks slack-mouthed confused.

She smiles a bland little victory smile. Then Max smiles wide and leans on the counter. She takes a half step back. Max leans closer. She takes a full step to the left. It's like some kind of dance. Max throws his head back, thrusts his arm in the air flamenco style, pulls a full upper plate of teeth out of his mouth, leans further over the counter, and palm up, offers his teeth to the young girl. "Ya see these teeth Ma'am? Got them in the U.S. Navy. See! That's my USN serial number and there's my name M. Biermann right there on the bridge. These teeth won't fit anyone else's mouth but mine… unless you want to give it a try honey." A quick step backward. Her eyes wide. Her part seems even wider now. Twenty-five bucks are thrown on the counter. I can see Max is beginning to enjoy this little encounter. With a flourish, he signs off for the money. I scoop it up and steer him out the door.

Given our condition when we go to the jail to spring Smiley we're lucky we don't get arrested. I have all I can do to keep Max's teeth in his goddamn mouth. It's like he discovered a key to the city or something. The cop on the desk is bored, but even his nose twitches a bit. Looks like he could use a drink. Smiley is a grizzled old cowboy with a chaw-stained beard. I like him.

We head for the flophouse. Jennette, the woman behind the desk, has a smoker's face and a road map of varicose veins exposed below a shapeless housedress. You get the feeling she hasn't smiled in a long time. She leads us up three flights and throws back a curtain that serves as a door. There is one bed with a thin suspicious looking mattress, a couple of wooden chairs, and a dirty sink with a missing hot water tap. The hopper and shower are down the hall.

Jennette comes back with a few scrawny blankets and throws them on the bed. "Alright boys! No fights. No fires. No fuckin' around. Unnerstand?"

When she leaves Max walks over to the sink and pisses in it. I'm not sure if he really has to relieve himself or whether he's just marking territory. Smiley wants to get down to business and volunteers to go get the hooch. He returns in a short time with a gallon jug of Wild Irish Rose. "Stronger than Thunderbird and all that other crap." he says. With him are two guys he met in jail earlier in the week. Smiley opens the bottle with a flourish and with a big smile introduces Thomas and William. They throw a little money onto the bed. I don't know it yet but this will be the high point of the evening; anticipating a night with an unlimited supply of booze.

After the bottle is passed around a few times, a skinny no-ass big belt buckle guy stumbles in. "Howdy folks! I'm Jim from across the hall. Looks like yawl got a nice little party goin'. Mind if I join in?" No one says yeah but no one says no. Jim throws a few coins on the bed, takes a couple of long swigs out of the bottle, belches as if that's part of the drinking deal and passes it to me. I am well past needing another swig and wave him off.

"No thanks."

No-ass Jim gives me a look. "Who's the kid?"

Max takes the bottle. "This is Jack. He's ok. Just up from Fort Sill. His daddy's a man of the road too." I didn't know I had a pedigree. Maybe everyone has one, one way or another. Max starts to pass the bottle on to Thomas.

Jim now gives Thomas a look. "You an Indian?"

"Yeah?"

"I knew it. A Cherokee. Am I right?

"What's it to you little man?"

"I don't drink with no Cherokees, especially when they're drunk!"

Thomas slowly gets to his feet; William right behind him.

Jim stumbles back and pulls a puny little jackknife, waving it back and forth. Looking to Max he hisses "Call off your dogs!"

Max grabs the jug by the neck and steps between the men. He leans over Jim. "Get the fuck out."

Jim backs toward the door still waving the knife. "Fuck you guys! I got a bottle of real whiskey, not the shit you and Tonto there been drinking." With that, he shuffles out.

Smiley turns to Thomas and William. "That's one troubled hombre. Have another drink, amigo." I think at that moment Smiley wishes he could speak Cherokee. What stuck in my mind was how fast all these guys got drunk, how fast and ugly they crashed, and how much schoolyard shit went on. I started to see my father in a different light.

The next morning, head banging and stomach churning, I ease past the snoring bodies and head for Fort Sill. I head out toward the highway with my thumb out. A hot red sports car zips by then screeches to a stop a ways up the road. Sometimes when this happens you run up the road so your ride doesn't have to wait, only to have the asshole peel out when you're almost to the car. So I'm grateful the stop was real. "Hey man, thanks for stopping."

The driver Hal shakes my hand "No problemo. Where you headed?"

"Lawton."

"You're in luck. I'm headed to Anadarko. What's your name?"

I am in luck. I always try to make conversation figuring whoever picks me up is bored and could use some company. Hal is an ABD (all but dissertation) epidemiologist studying venereal disease among Native American males. He is amazed that I'm familiar with Hans Zinsser's book *Rats, Lice and History* (I don't tell him I only bought it because of the neat title). The main point of the book is we're creating super germs that survive 1000 degree steam in hospital laundries, flies that get fat on DDT, virus permutations for which there is no vaccine, meanwhile public health programs keep people alive in the gene pool who would have died young in a more Darwinian environment. The conclusion? A pandemic is just a matter of time. Hal absolutely cackles when I tell him about my "Cracked Plate Theory" which states that according to an old wives' tale, cracks in plates harbor deadly germs. Therefore, in order to keep our gene pool filled with folks packed with tough, no-nonsense white blood cell warriors we should all eat off cracked plates and let Darwin have his way. I was hoping this conversation might get me all the way to Fort Sill but it was not to be. When we get to Chickasha, I realize hitching to Fort Sill would be better from Chickasha than from Anadarko and you can only talk about rats, lice, and even history for so long. As we pull up to the one traffic light in town I grab my duffle bag, start to thank Hal and open the car door. He looks surprised and reaches across the seat. I reach out to shake his hand but he grabs for my crotch. I jump out of the car.

Everything happened so fast. But standing by the road waiting for the next ride I'm thinking about how naïve I am. I mean the guy had a polished wood penis on his stick shift. *Am I dumb or what?* On the way back to post I'm thinking about my father and what I learned this weekend about his life or lack of it. I know he's smarter than those guys in OK City but I'm thinking in a lot of ways I'm older than he is, or more like he's younger than I am.

DRIVING UNCLE SAM

The sweat rings under their arms and on their backs grew with each push. Every time I popped the clutch the grunts and nasty looks grew louder. Jesus, it was hot! I had just landed in Georgia from Fort

Hood, Texas to participate in a two-week training exercise called Swift Strike III—a $10M (in 1964 dollars) exercise which involved 70,000 GIs pitting the 101st Airborne from Fort Campbell, Kentucky and the 5th Mechanized Division from Fort Reilly, Colorado against the 82nd airborne from Fort Bragg, North Carolina and the 2nd Infantry Division from Fort Benning, Georgia. I think they were trying to determine if it would be better to start wars in countries with nice AAA road maps rather than muck about in backward places where it's so easy to get lost or stuck in the mud. They also may have been trying to determine which airborne division was the flat-out nuttiest.

I was not there to fight or even pretend fight. I was really there to get out of Fort Sill, Oklahoma. My superiors wanted me out almost as bad as I wanted to get out and I often made it clear that I wanted to be out real bad. They saw me as a negative influence in the company. Actually, my negative influence was pretty puny stuff. (See the "100% Honest" story below for more details.) At any rate, they volunteered me to go to Georgia to drive Air Force pilots around. The flyboys' job was to determine how many troops were napalmed or strafed after jets flew over at tree top height. You couldn't hear them coming but once past they made a terrific roar. It drove home to me the realization that in a real war your chances of staying alive didn't have a hell of a lot to do with how good you could shoot or how strong and brave you were.

Here I was almost twenty-one years old, about to drive guys who could fly planes faster than the speed of sound a few feet above tree tops and I didn't know how to drive a car. No one born south of Philadelphia believed I could not drive. They thought I was a malingerer or worse, a New Yorker. But, I had a plan. The Artillery unit I was in at Fort Sill was going to Germany. Without wasting much time on research or arithmetic, I figured after I got discharged in Germany, I would buy a Mercedes, drive it around Europe, ship it home, sell it for a fortune in the US and buy an American car. For this I would need a military license. I was the only warm body in the unit who didn't know how to drive, so off to driver's school I went.

The first two mornings were pretty tough. We sat on backless benches in a windowless, airless basement watching WWII convoy films for three hours each day. What I learned was this: taillights on the back of convoy vehicles are made up of four small lights (cat's eyes). If you see four distinct lights you're probably too close. If the four lights appear to be two lights you're ok. If the four lights look like one light you better haul ass trooper. That's it. Six hours of educational film more painful than even the infamous dental hygiene and venereal disease films. I thought about the guy in the movie *Stalag 17* who painted eyeballs on his eyelids and slept through all the Nazi lectures.

On the third day we went out to the driving range—no not golf—and practiced with deuce-and-a-halfs (two and a half ton trucks). It was scary but fun. These were pretty big trucks but the good news was that they were slush buckets (automatic shifts), so all you had to do was aim the sonofabitch where you wanted to go, step on the gas and go. Sure we had to drive over dicey make-shift bridges and steep grades but it didn't take long to get the hang of it. That night I dreamed of Mercedes, German beer, and Frauleins.

The next day was much more challenging. The M38 WWII jeeps we had were much smaller and maneuverable than the deuce-and-a-halfs but they were stick shifts. Lucky for me the Spec 2 (Specialist 2nd grade) tester in the jeep with me was one of the coolest guys I met in the Army.

We're at the foot of a very steep grade. The jeep is bucking like a bronco at the Calgary Stampede. It's so bad the Spec 2 asks me if I don't want a license. I say "fuck no I want a license real bad" and start mumbling about Mercedes, beer, and Frauleins. "So you want to pass this test?" "Fuckin' A, Man!" With that he slid his leg over mine put his foot on the clutch grabbed the handbrake and told me to hit the gas when he said to. Well, it took a few more bucks to get in synch but before long we were one hell of a jeep driving duo and I got my military license. I still feel guilty that I can't remember this guy's name. A truly decent human being.

The flight from Fort Hood was a bitch. We were on a huge cargo plane carrying five jeeps, a handful of officers, some noncoms (non-commissioned officers) and five enlisted drivers. The officers and senior noncoms knew the drill and grabbed all the blankets. The rest of us froze our asses in what felt like the longest flight in history. But it didn't take long to thaw out on that Georgia tarmac.

My jeep was last off the plane. All the other jeeps rolled down the ramp and started right up. My jeep made it down the ramp but didn't start. I pressed my foot on the starter button on the floor harder. One of the sergeants mumbled something about the altitude change and told me to pump the gas pedal a few times, which I did—nothing. Another sergeant established his superiority. "Hell Sarge! It ain't a fuel problem. The goddam starter motor ain't made a peep. It's probably a "battry" problem. We need to jump start this here "vee-hic-al." There were no jumper cables to be found which in hindsight might have been my first tiny step toward simulating the chaos of real war. Then another sergeant established his superiority. He motioned toward jeep number four "Hey, soldier, back your jeep up against this one and give it a push. But then, a Chief Warrant Officer established his superiority. "No way, sergeant! I'm responsible for these brand new M151 babies. Gonna evaluate them during this war game. We're not gonna put a scratch on 'em till they seen some real action." With that he then established his leadership skills by getting behind my jeep and shouting "Let's go, boys!" Even the Officers had to man-up to this front-line democracy.

I got pushed all over that tarmac. They pushed and I popped the clutch, push and pop, push and pop. Finally a Major said "Son, let me give it a try." "Yes, sir!" He got in and of course it started right up. No push needed. Purred like a kitten. They all looked at the jeep then all turned to look at me.

All was quiet. Heat was shimmering off the tarmac. I thought I saw the Russian navy glittering in the distance but I kinda knew it was wishful thinking. I could feel my troublemaking shit eating grin starting its nervous trip from my churning stomach up to my stricken face. I knew I had to act fast. I tried to make it sound like that major had magical powers. "Gee, sir, what did you do?" The major leaned his face in closer and spoke slowly, quietly, with every syllable a well-enunciated hiss that boomed in my ears. "Well, Private," He somehow made the word "private" an expletive. What I heard was more along the lines of: "Well, you worthless piece of shit!"

"Well, Private, I fuckin' walked over to this fuckin' jeep, sat my fuckin' ass in the fuckin' driver's seat, put one fuckin' foot on the fuckin' clutch, the other fuckin' foot on the fuckin' gas pedal and pushed the fuckin' starter button with this fuckin' little finger!" He proceeded to stick the finger mentioned about an inch from my nose. I was confused. *Why wouldn't he use his foot to start the ...* Before I could finish that thought he swept his arm toward the dash board and pushed a button. Again, the jeep started right up.

"Oh! So what's that button on the floor ... sir?"

"That's the fuckin' high beam. Where'd you learn to drive ... Private?"

"Fort Sill, sir!"

"When? Last week?" he asked with venomous sarcasm.

I savored this moment. The ball was in my court. "You are correct sir! Last week sir. The starter button there was on the floor for those Fort Sill jeeps, sir! I guess we got nothing but the very-best for these war games, sir!"

He slumped ever so slightly. The hiss was now a tired sigh of deflation. I learned that playing dumb or even being dumb in the Army, at least the peacetime Army, is a useful survival skill. The breeze in that open jeep driving back to the barracks felt great.

SOUND OFF

Long before the term *"went viral"* went viral, our military provided a hotbed of slang. The name "Uncle Sam" goes all the way back to the War of 1812. Military slang has become a standard part of our vocabulary. Most of it's profane, some poetic. Even SNAFU (Situation Normal All Fucked Up) can be heard on Main Street and in board rooms. Some folks think it's "All Fouled Up" All I can say to that is "Those fuckin' jerkoffs got their heads up their ass!" For some phrases, time has stripped the bones bare. For example, "You bet your fuckin' ass" has evolved to "fuckin' A," an efficient form of hearty affirmation.

Some phrases have lived mercifully short lives. For example, when I was in the Army in the early 1960s *"I got the ass"* meant "I'm angry." I knew this leaden expression was to be short lived when I overheard a mess hall verbal duet between two lifer cooks that went something like this.

"Hey! What the hell's wrong with you? You got the ass or somethin?"

"Yeah! I got the ass."

"Why you got the ass?"

"I'll tell you why I got the ass! I got the ass 'cause you got the ass 'cause I got the ass! Asshole!"

Besides giving me the ass, that discussion got me thinking. Although I did get plenty of time to think in that peacetime Army, I seldom took advantage. But this time I ended up betting a beer with my buddy Allen Brown that I could go for two weeks using only three phrases: "Fuck it" "No big thing" and "This is true." To get my morning sausage gravy over toast (affectionately known as SOS—Shit On a Shingle), I merely had to point and say "Fuck it." A smile would get me a look of pity and an extra helping of the grayish treat. When my mess mate on pots & pans exclaimed "We're gonna be here all goddam night" I would fake a Zen-like calm and intone "No big thing." When he would come back with "They're goddam tryin' to kill us!" "This is true."

Did I enjoy that beer? Fuckin' A!

100% HONEST

I was lying on my bunk listening to the grass die in the heavy black Oklahoma night when I got called to the colonel's office.

"At ease, private. I just called you in to ascertain why you have not contributed to the Fort Sill United Fund Drive. Did you know that you are the only soldier in the entire regiment who has failed to do so?"

"No, sir!"

"Well, I'm proud to say that ever since I took command of The Fighting Six of the Ninth Artillery Regiment we have had a record 100% participation."

What he did not say was in this peacetime army, about the only things on which officers were evaluated were the number of troops under his command that were involved in off-post auto accidents and the percent participation in the United Fund Drive.

"Well' sir, I have not donated because I get paid $22 a month most of which I send home to my mother."

The colonel stood, dug for his wallet in his starched and creased fatigues, pulled out a dollar bill and laid it on the corner of his desk and said "Private, your mother must be proud to have such a good son." Then, pointing to the bill, "I'm glad to help you out."

I knew I had him. "But sir, that wouldn't be honest. Would it?"

CALIFORNIA DREAMIN'

Jack with guitar, "California Dreaming" in CT. Circa 1966.

After my discharge from the Army in 1964 I traveled a bit and found myself in a seedy hotel in the Tenderloin section of San Francisco. Seedy was a kind description. Seedy also described my overall physical, mental, and financial condition. I had limited options and, staying in my room was not going to be one of them. Besides, it was Saturday night in Frisco! I needed a plan and an ad in the San Francisco Chronicle got my attention. It said that tonight, a drive-in in Oakland had an all-night show featuring the hot new film *2001: A Space Odyssey* along with a night full of cartoons and psychedelic music, "Bring your sleeping bag."

The last time I brought a sleeping bag to an all-night event was the Annual Easter Pageant hosted by Fort Sill, Oklahoma. The pageant consisted of a series of tableaux, sort of like a PowerPoint depiction of the Crucifixion and Resurrection of Jesus. I didn't see much of the show. A young lady named Marla settled down next to me after setting a throng of lively young Christians free to roam the pageant. We got to talking. I couldn't believe my luck. I thought, *maybe it's the sweater my sister sent me*. She called it Scandia, the latest thing in knitting. It looked like it was made from wool rope – something a homeless Norwegian might wear. But I was pretty sure this was the only Scandia sweater west of the Hudson.

As cool as that sweater was, I started to get cold. Marla suggested we share her sleeping bag. Now don't get me wrong. This was an Easter pageant for Christ sake! We were surrounded by thousands of Christians. A little cuddling, a little smooching, this was the closest to heaven I got that night. I didn't even mind that I picked up a case of crabs (yes lice) from Marla's sleeping bag. I figured if that was all night Easter in Oklahoma, what was an all-night California drive-in Space Odyssey going to be like? I was psyched! I had a plan.

I stuff a sleeping bag in my duffle bag and head out. The drive-in address is 197843 International Blvd in Oakland. After getting directions from mostly helpless and hopeless well-meaning people in the Tenderloin, I catch a bus to Oakland. Downtown I transfer to the bus that will take me to the drive-in. As we swing through the city, the streets get more crowded—mostly Black people. The project I grew up in was mostly Black, the Army was mostly Black. So I'm ok but am mindful that things can go south even here in the West. We roll south until I'm the only one on the bus. The bus driver keeps checking me out in the mirror. I bet he thinks I'm going to rob him. Finally he stops the bus, gives me a smirky little smile and calls out "End of line, all out!" I show him the ad. "Hell man, that's another six/seven miles south." It's getting dark. The bus driver realizes I'm too lost to rob him, he heads back north. As we ride back the crowds start to pick up again—only a little thicker now. I'm the only white person on the bus until this stringy blond haired kid gets on. He's wearing cutoff jeans, tee shirt, and flip flops. That's all! I figure, *Hey this is California*. But I can see he's pretty agitated. Sweat mats his stringy hair and tee shirt, his face is splotchy. He looks around the bus, and heads straight for me. The bus driver swings around in his seat. "Hey kid, ya gotta pay the fare now." "I just got robbed man! Two Black guys."

The bus driver must figure this is no place to make Blondie get out of the bus. Blondie sits next to me and almost shouts "I just got robbed man! Two Black guys." I nod. I must look sympathetic. He nods back. I'm just glad he's not saying the N word. We continue toward downtown and pull up at a crowded intersection with about twenty people waiting to get on the bus. Blondie jumps up, points out the window and shouts "Hey man there's the Black dude who robbed me!" That's the first time I hear the word 'Dude.' Still don't like it but *Hey, this is California.*

Some people have already boarded. The bus driver shuts and locks the door and calls the police on a walkie-talkie kind of phone. The folks outside the bus don't know what's going on except that this white driver won't let them on the Goddamn bus. It doesn't take long for them to reach the banging on the bus stage. People on the bus demand to be let off. The noise is starting to attract guys just hanging out sharing a little taste. Robber Dude is still in line. He has yet to figure out why the bus driver won't open the door. For the first time in my life I'm glad to see flashing lights and hear sirens as the police cruiser pulls up in front of the bus. The crowd quickly calms down. Our cities have not yet started to burn. The cop puts Blondie in his cruiser, Robber Dude finally figures out what's happening and quickly disappears. I pray the cop doesn't chase him. The bus fills and heads to Oakland's center. I catch the last bus back to San Francisco.

By the time I get to my hotel, the front door is locked. So much for fire code. After banging for a while I head for the bus station. At this time of night, it doesn't take long for a cop to check me out. I tell him my story. He can see by my army issue duffle bag and combat boots that I just got out of the Army or maybe he wants to make sure he doesn't have to fill out a homicide report on his shift. He drives me to the neighborhood precinct house and lets me sleep in an empty holding cell. Good thing I got my own sleeping bag. No crabs.

Forty years later I finally get to watch *2001: A Space Odyssey*. All I can say is "What?"

7

CAT & DOGS

Jacky and Snoopy. Circa 1970.

"Please Dad! Please! Can we have a dog? Please! You had dogs. Why can't we." This was a constant refrain from my kids' early childhood years. A highlight in my life as a parent came when my then 13-year-old son Brendan looked at me in his wise-beyond-his-years look and said "Hey Dad, thanks for not letting me get a dog."

I always had dogs. Then I had kids, six of them. For about twenty years I said "No" to constant pleas from my kids to get a dog. So they never got to enjoy the joys of distemper, dysplasia, rabies, heart worm, Parvovirus, fleas, flea bombs, ticks, Lyme Disease, mange, dog food, picking up still-warm processed dog food, house breaking, shedding, wandering, skunks, porcupines, running deer, electric dog fences, rolling on rotted roadkill, leashes, runs, non-stop barking, kennels, choke collars, lost dog posters, doggies in heat, child humpers, crotch sniffers, car chasers, muddy paws, spaying, shots, professional grooming and $300 tooth brushing, vet bills, to say nothing of chewed *slippers and hearing aids—yes, hearing aids. Even naming a dog can ruin a relationship.*

A firm hypocritical "No" saved me a bunch of time, money, and aggravation. Some may say I am a hypocrite for not letting my kids have dogs when as a kid I had several of my own. They are correct. In my book, hypocrisy ranks high on the ladder of parental perfection. It requires a level of enlightened acceptance that is seldom attained. So go ahead. Share with your kids the details of what you smoked, ingested, and had sex with when you were their age. Go ahead! Be their friend. Recently I asked Brendan why he thanked me for not letting him get a dog. He thought for a moment, smiled and said "Distemper, dysplasia, rabies, heart worm, Parvovirus, fleas, ticks…

MICKEY: MY FIRST DOG

When I was nine, Butchie Bavarskis and I took three buses to get to the then high class suburb of Wethersfield, Connecticut to choose from a basketful of cuddly squirming miracles. We each picked from the sweetest litter of seven pups god ever created. They were a Beagle/English Setter mix with curly white fur, black and tan markings, long soft ears, big floppy feet to grow into, and the brownest deepest most loving eyes. I held my breath as Butchie, who was three years older than me, picked first. To my great relief, he passed over the hands-down most beautiful, intelligent, noble pup ever born.

I named him Mickey. Don't know why. Five bucks each and two cardboard boxes thrown in to carry our very own pups, our new life-long buddies back home to Hartford's North End. If Norman Rockwell had been on that bus we would have been on the cover of *The Saturday Evening Post*. The pups had everyone smiling. We kids probably had something to do with those smiles too. One old timer wasn't smiling. "Nice dogs. Too bad they won't make it in the city." Well, I'd show that wrinkled old sourpuss.

Six weeks later Mickey, frothing at the mouth died of distemper. About that time, I read a book *The Sorghum Grows High* about Catholic missionary priests in China. So, I made a plan. I would become a missionary or maybe even a saint, go to heaven and get back with Mickey.

This plan lasted about two years until Jesus and I parted ways. But, while it lasted, it kept me out of trouble—out of big trouble anyway.

Happy

As time went by, I added new dogs to my "Love Forever" dog list. Happy, whose full name was Half Past Eleven because a little white spot on his chest kept him from being called Midnight, was a feisty little mongrel. He got hit by a car outside Saint Michael's School. The news spread through school while I was in choir class.

Choir class was universally hated—at least by the boys—until one day Sister Emilianna shouted in a rare display of musical passion "Stand on the balls of your feet boys. On the balls!" That's it. That's all it took for fifth grade boys bored out of their minds to elevate that simple command into a year-long mantra anytime things got slow.

I was a canary which was pretty high on the pecking order of student warblers. It was not the highest ranking but I was glad I was not a robin. They were basically told to keep their goddamn mouths shut. When class ended it didn't take long for the news about Jacky Barry's dog to find me. I ran out of the school. Happy's body lay stiff in the gutter, a flattened broken body with an eye protruding from his skull. I wish I could say I gave Happy a proper burial, but no. I ran home as fast as I could.

Mack

A few weeks later Father McDonald showed up at the house with a new dog. Father Mack was what we called a regular guy. If kids got in a fight, he would bring them over to the church basement and have them duke it out with real boxing gloves. He wore sweatshirts more often than the collar which solidified his standing as a regular guy. Remember this was the fifties. You didn't have to stray very far off the line to be labeled different. We named the dog Mack after Father Mack.

Mack was mostly Airedale. These dogs are bred to hunt lions and tigers. They're fearless, aggressive and crazy. Not a good dog for a kid who only wanted to have a tail wagging buddy. We played basketball nearly every day at the project playground. Every work day at five o'clock

Johnny Zeph walked through the playground on his way home from work. Actually he didn't walk, he lurched. Left foot forward right foot swinging a half circle Frankenstein. It drove Mack crazy. Mack's dog brain must have told him here was wounded prey. Easy pickings. But Johnny got pretty good with his cane and when he connected with Mack, he would turn and curse us. We just laughed, oblivious to the pain and humiliation behind those curses after a long day's work. Finally Mack got farmed out to a farmer who could use a real mean dog.

GOODBYE SNOOPY

I had a dog I didn't much like, a Basset Hound. He was spoiled and cantankerous when I got him. I had just moved to Vermont when my girlfriend, Elizabeth, brought him up from Connecticut. His owner fed him buttered toast from the table and seldom took him outside. They even named him Snoopy! I should have known right from the start.

When Snoopy first set foot in the Vermont house, I heard a racket on the porch, looked out to see this squirming tan and white sausage. Stubby little turtle legs flailing away making sounds like Spanish castanets. It turns out his nails are way long because he's never been let out of the house. I open the door and bend down to greet him but he scrambles through the door, circles the kitchen, runs into the parlor, lifts his leg, and pisses on the couch. I don't know, maybe another dog pissed on it in the past. Nevertheless I grab a newspaper to let this dog know that in Vermont you don't piss on someone's couch unless they ask you to.

I give him a little slap with a thin rural newspaper, fully expecting him to tell me in dog body language that he now understands about Vermont couches and will never do it again. Instead he bares his teeth, a nasty little bare tooth smile and lets out a long multikey bone-chilling hound dog howl before returning to the smile. Until then I'm not thinking too much about the skunks that live in the woodshed which is attached Vermont-style to the kitchen. I don't know how many skunks cut loose but my eyes start to burn. I didn't sleep well that night.

Snoopy doesn't whine to be let out, he shakes his head. His flapping ears sound like a runaway window shade. I look forward to getting to know my new dog and introduce him to the great Vermont outdoors.

He's on a leash because I'm afraid he may take off for the land of buttered toast. We're not out more than five minutes when an Arnold Schwarzenegger of a German shepherd comes bounding up. Snoopy growls and gives him that toothy smile. The hairs on the big dog's back starts to stand as he returns the smile. His fangs look much larger than ours. I haul Snoopy back into the house. The German Shepherd hangs around for a couple more days while I try to figure out how to house break a dog that can't leave the house.

Anyway that was the first few days. Things did settle down, but never completely. Snoopy was an opportunist. One day he nabbed a Popsicle from my five-year-old nephew. I chased him but he wolfed it down before I could get to him. One night months later his gagging and retching woke me. This was nothing new. He would eat anything. When I went to clean up his mess, I found the popsicle stick he snatched four months earlier.

One of his hobbies was running away. Unfortunately, after a week or so, he was always returned. In all fairness, he was useful at times. I loved to lie on the floor, cover my eyes with one of his ears and nap. It was even better than those little warm eye baggies you get in some of the better yoga classes. So Snoopy wasn't all bad, just mostly bad.

One day he seemed to have trouble breathing. The vet gave him some medicine and sent us home. That night his breathing got more labored and he did something he seldom did. He tried to follow me around. I put him in the car to bring him to the vet. By then he could not breath lying down. He sat in the front seat watching me closely. I scratched his ears. He died before we got to the vet. It was hard to say goodbye.

NORWEGIAN AND AMERICAN DOGS

I grew up at a time when it was easy to believe America was the greatest country in the world in every aspect of life. Travel can reinforce that view but more often contradicts it. On a train from Bergen to Stavanger, Norway a man stepped aboard carrying a newspaper and a limp dog leash. I thought this was a bit odd until I saw a dog follow the man to his seat and lie down on the floor under the man's feet. The man paid little attention to the dog and started reading the paper. I half expected the man to share the news with the dog.

Back in the day, whenever I saw a girl with a dog I would cringe. And, if the dog had a bandanna I would run. Run out of the commune, dorm, barn, tent, yurt, geodesic dome, crib, whatever. Why? Because, these dogs were always totally out of control and would be shot on sight and eaten in more civilized societies.

It's a slow rainy afternoon on a commune in Vermont's Northeast Kingdom. Neil Young's *Harvest* album along with a generous bag of recently harvested home-grown Vermont Green is helping us through the afternoon mellows. A dog named after some Tolkien character comes romping into the room, sniffs every crotch, lifts its leg, and pisses on a girl's genuine leather Mexican hand-tooled psychedelic backpack. The girl who owns the backpack breaks through the mellow fog of communal well-being and shrieks "Do you know how fucking much that genuine leather Mexican hand-tooled psychedelic backpack cost?" The girl who owns the dog takes a hit on a passing bong then offers "Ya know, another dog must have already pissed on your backpack. Samwise just wanted to say hello too." Unfortunately, there was no gun in the genuine leather Mexican hand-tooled psychedelic backpack.

SHAME US

Shame Us was an Irish Setter. Her mother and father were pedigree AKC royalty registered as Adam and Eve. That's "Evening's Mischief Maker" and "Adam's Mourning Apple," thank you. I didn't realize at the time how lucky I was to have a pure bred dog that was actually worth a damn.

Shame Us, the dog. Circa 1973.

The fact that she was not only a pure breed but a pure breed Irish Setter to boot made the odds far more unlikely that she would be worth a damn. But, worth a damn she was. Best dog I ever had. She even had a brain which made her unique among Irish Setters and many other pure breeds as well. I mean, some of these pooches are lucky they can walk, and those breeds that need to be carried give one pause as to imagine how they can procreate.

There were two little guys who ran a grocery store on the way into town. I didn't like going there but they had a great meat section. You could see that these guys were not twins but it was remarkable how they were ugly in the same way. Somehow their appearance and deportment created an irrational anxiety in me.

So, maybe that's why I had such a visceral reaction when two beagles showed up the exact minute that Shame Us went into heat. Of course! Beagles! Those two meat guys looked like Beagles. Maybe they are Beagles, come to deflower Shame Us. Well fuck that! I'll burn their goddam store—London broils and all!

Did you ever wage a war on dogs? I don't recommend it. The conventional wisdom says it's good for a female dog to have a litter of pups before they are spayed. Of course, hottie Shame Us didn't help. She just wanted to get laid. It didn't matter to her if she got humped by a goddam pygmy Beagle from Mars.

Anyway, after the dogs left, Shame Us started putting on weight. I still don't know how it happened. Some folks still believe in the Immaculate Conception. Hey! You never know. What I do know is that Shame Us delivered thirteen beautiful Setter/Beagle pups. We thought it was just another miracle!

We went to a funeral in Connecticut and came home to find her lying at the front door. She was old and declining enough to say that it was her time to go. It looked like she passed a stone of some type. She must have been in great pain and was looking for us. I cried.

Shame Me.

I can't picture Heaven without my dogs, but I can't picture them in Heaven either. Will they be Heaven broken? Will there be trees or hydrants? How old will each of them be? Will they hump each other or fight to see who is the alpha dog? Will they run deer? Are there deer in Heaven? It's hard to picture Heaven. But, if there is a Heaven, Shame Us will be there to greet me, even if it's on my way to some other place.

SPOT THE CAT

This cat story would take up too much time. I don't much like cats anyway. Okay! Okay!

Here's a cat story. I had a cat that was all black except for a white spot on her chest. Many friends and neighbors thought the little white fur spot looked nice. I thought it looked like a hand grenade.

DOG LESSONS LEARNED

Dogs are not furniture or toys. You can't stick them in some desk drawer when you're finished playing with them. Don't give loved ones or even unloved ones gift pets. Giving someone a shit load of responsibility is not a gift. Don't shake hands with dogs, not even if you are never going to wear pantyhose or white jeans again. Dogs do not understand the concept of love. They do understand the concept of pack hierarchy. So get a dog AFTER you fix your marriage.

Hippie Chickens

I'm standing in the front yard of my farm in NH. My buddy Dave is lending me Cream's great album "Wheels of Fire." I hear this commotion out back. My nephew Tommy is screaming the scream of a terrified two-year-old. Roy Rooster is also emitting some testosterone-fueled teenage rooster victory screech. I run out back to see Roy Rooster, claws out, jumping up and down on a prostrate, still screaming Tommy. I whack Roy on the run with all my might. Good thing "Wheels of Fire" is a double album. Roy goes down like a brick. I'm holding Tommy close. In a few minutes, still laying on his side, Roy opens the one eye I can see and blinks. The sonofabitch is still alive and I can't figure out what he's thinking. He just lays there blink-blink, blink-blink.

I don't know for sure if the trauma changed Tommy's life. He now works with brown bears in Alaska. He often gets within a few feet of them. But, based on many years of experience and a strict protocol at McNeil River Bear Sanctuary, the bears don't associate Tommy or any other human with food, sex, or danger. But me, right now, I'm getting out of this chicken business.

We got Roy Rooster this past week to bring some order to the chicken coop. You know, a nice little dictatorship, a bit of fascism. This was years before Trump and Proud Boys were invented. I already got way too many male chickens. Did you ever hear a teenage rooster crow? Jesus! It makes you want to strangle them all. The tools that came with the farm included a capon-making kit but I don't have the balls to mess with that stuff.

And for the past two winters what do I get? Frozen water, frozen chicken shit, but no eggs. Then, just as the spring snow starts to soften up, dogs come around. What do these dumb birds do? They fly the coop, stick their heads in the snow, asses pointed to the sun and suffocate or have heart attacks, or something goofy like that. The dogs really enjoy it. I tell my buddy Joe, I'm getting out of the chicken business.

Joe is an old high school friend from Hartford who is living with me, my mother, and my part-time girlfriend on the farm I bought in New Hampshire. When Joe was in high school he dressed almost as dapper as the Black dudes at Weaver High School. Something happened when he went to art school at the University of Hartford. At a time when we all were earnestly trying to become bohemians, Joe became our first hippie. He even went to Haight Ashbury before any of us ever heard of it. He studied astrology, witchcraft, tie dye shirts, and chemicals that fry the brain. He was one of the first guys in Hartford to sport a long beard, hair down to his ass, and sandals. Joe was able to pull this life-style switcheroo because he was about six foot two and weighed 130 pounds at best. Folks just gawked. Funny how times change.

My mother doesn't like Joe because he has dope delivered to our house by US mail. My mother thinks that will get me in trouble. I have a good job at Dartmouth College. She's right but back then, I was a bit of an asshole too. Anyway, after Joe hears of my quitting chickens, he decides to help me out. Never having been in the corporate world, he never heard the admonition "No surprise is a good surprise."

It's a rare 95 degree scorcher in New Hampshire. I come home from work to find Joe soaked in sweat, shaking from exhaustion, and hallucinating. All he could talk about was the chicken who disappeared. He knew it was pure and simple witchcraft! For sure!

So what happened? First off Joe collects the tools he figures he needs to dispatch the unwanted chickens, this includes: an empty fifty-five gallon steel drum, a wood pallet, a three foot length of 3/4 inch copper tubing, about seven feet of electric fence wire, a machete, a square foot or so of cardboard, and some chicken feed.

Next, he assembles the tools in a manner that will enable him to mercifully kill the chickens without ever touching them. He places the fifty-five gallon drum on the pallet; he doubles the fence wire and runs it through the copper tubing using the slack to fashion a handle on one end and a noose on the other; he then places the cardboard with chicken feed on it just outside the drum and next to the machete.

Now he starts the process that will fill my freezer with much despised but tasty chickens. It takes a bit of a chase but Joe finally gets the noose over a chicken's head and gently places the chicken under the barrel and removes the noose. I know, I know. He can garrote that chicken right then and there, but, he sticks to the plan. He grabs the machete in one hand while slowly tipping the barrel. Sure enough, the chicken makes a few of those ditzy little chicken head motions and spies the feed. I don't know when that chicken last ate or whether or not it's hungry but it herky jerks its ditzy head toward the feed. Joe now has that sucker right where he wants him. He wastes no time. That machete comes down with all the force a modern 130 pound American male can deliver. Joe's heart races. He opens his eyes. No head! Where's the goddam head? He lifts the barrel. What the fuck? No head! No chicken! Joe spends the rest of the day chasing chickens and consulting tarot cards.

The next morning I sleep late and when I come down my mother is smiling. She's baking some Irish bread for my buddy Art Romano who just rode up from Connecticut on his motorcycle. While he's waiting for me to wake up, he kills and dresses all the chickens.

"Hey Art, Thanks for all your help with the chickens."

"No problem Jack. But ya know, one of the chickens had one hell of a gash on the top of its neck. Never saw anything like it."

Art grew up on a real farm.

HOME AGAIN, HOME AGAIN, JIGGITY JOG

8

LOVE & MARRIAGE

Gerry, love of my life. 1979.

A MESSAGE TO PARADISE

Dear Mr. and Mrs. Ryan,

Sorry I could not reach you both before this. I just subscribed to this new Paradise Mail thing this week. So for my first message sent as your son-in-law, I want to thank you both for all you have done for me. You have done the best thing anyone ever did for me.

Thank you, Mr. Ryan. Thank you for teaching your kids love and devotion in the face of sorrow and despair. It could not have been easy to tell six kids, the youngest eleven the oldest nineteen, that their mother was dead. It could not have been easy to devote the rest of your life to raising them, keeping them together, and grieving your own loss—alone. And you knew plenty about loss. Your brother, a wonderful priest who was an everyday part of the family died within months of your wife. You buried your first born infant. You saw your oldest son bury his beautiful twelve year old daughter.

And Jim, you saw your own mother killed by a train after making sure you were out of that car stalled on the tracks. And, in the aftermath, you saw your brother and sister farmed out to relatives. What did you do with all that loss? You turned it into strength. A strength that enabled you to put one foot in front of the other, and, come what may, keep your kids together. Those six kids learned valuable lessons—not from what you said but by what you did. Each in their own way, reflect those lessons to this very day.

Times were different then. The day before the funeral Gerry remembers being shocked that the stores in downtown Providence were still open. "Don't they know my mother died?" All six went back to school the day after the funeral; Johnny, all the way back to college in Vermont; and you back to work. They stuck together. Still do. Still all together but, not too together, all good people, but not too good. I'm glad to be one of them.

Thank you, Mrs. Ryan. I am sorry I never got to meet you, but as life's experiences accumulate I feel I know you more and more. Your daughter, your namesake Geraldine was only fifteen when you died. I would not meet her for another fifteen years. And when I did, when I said "Yes! Yes! She's the one. Yes!" I was happy but I didn't really know what I was getting. I had no clue. Had never before seen how good it could be, would be!

There was a little restaurant in Englewood, Florida called "Food Is Love." I think of Gerry every time I saw that sign. It's not just because she is a fabulous cook, or that she can make a gourmet meal from whatever is left in the fridge, or that she always finds a way to accommodate extra company be they carnivores, vegetarians, or vegans. It's also because she makes it look easy. It looks easy because she loves what she's doing. And it's not just food. For her: family is love, friends are love, the guy bagging groceries at the store is love. A while back we were in a Cambridge restaurant. A young man from India was our waiter. Gerry asked simple questions. Where are you from? How many brothers and sisters? Within minutes they were hugging. He was crying. I was still coping with the wine list.

The Barry Family. Circa 2008.

Clearly Gerry loves life. She is currently learning American Sign Language because she "loves the beauty of the language." She goes to Patriot's practices in Foxboro because she loves Tom Brady. She now has library cards, in Englewood, Florida; Plainfield, New Hampshire; Dingle, Ireland; and all over Rhode Island. Every day Gerry continues to amaze. And every day, Mrs. Ryan, I learn a bit more about you. You are part of her and I am the better for it. I thank you for Gerry, for the special person she is.

PS: Please let me know if you get this. This is my first try at Paradise Mail and I usually screw these things up.

Gerry's Choices

I notice that a good number of folks look at me funny when I tell them that my wife Gerry makes most of the big decisions in our family. I don't mind saying this, because it's a fact. I'm not ashamed. Gerry makes good decisions. For example, she decided to buy the house we live in. "Big deal" you may say but we have lived in this house now for more than thirty years, and plan on staying right through to the very end and maybe even beyond.

She decided to give birth to four boys. A wonderful family any spouse would be proud of. Then, she decided to take in foster kids. She taught them to bond. She made a difference in their lives. Our stint in foster care led inevitably to the decision to adopt two of our foster girls. And as a bonus, watching Gerry in action will make our four boys better parents.

She decided to home school our kids, back when we were just about the only folks in town who did it. Home schooling started about thirty years ago and we're still at it. We can't claim to know whether or not the kids would be better prepared for life if they went to school, but I know how wonderful it was that the family could travel whenever we wanted to learn something because we were interested in it, and yes, the kids could learn to make their own decisions just like their mother does.

Gerry decided to say yes when I asked her to marry me although we knew each other only a few months and, as a thirty-seven year old bachelor, I was not exactly Mr. Commitment. This time I made the best decision of all when I asked her to marry me.

Gerry and Jack under arches at Kinney Azalea Gardens. 2019.

9

LITTLE RHODY

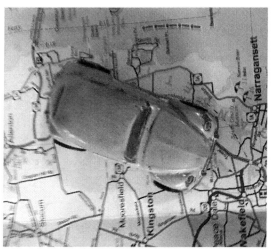

VW Bug from Barry children's Matchbox car
collection. Circa 2007.

SOUTH COUNTY RANT

There I was, lost in Rhode Island. It was 1972 and I was out exploring my new state. I now knew that Arctic was a village in the town of West Warwick. I considered heading to Providence to check out Neutaconkanut Hill. I think that's Algonquin for "Hill of Squirrels" but I remembered my mother telling me that Smith Hill was also loaded with squirrels and other politicians. So I decided to circumnavigate the Providence Plantations instead.

It looked simple enough. Just head east from Arctic, find the Bay, turn right and head for the ocean. At the ocean turn right again and head home to Weekapaug.

Are you with me so far? I know that sounds a bit condescending, but I have learned not to take directional aptitude for granted in the Ocean State.

This shortcoming is somewhat of a surprise given that our forbearers could find slaves in Africa, rum in the Caribbean, and whales in the southern oceans with impressive alacrity. So, at some time in our history, folks actually did know north from south although there is little evidence that they ever figured out right from wrong.

At any rate, I knew I lived on Waxcadowa Avenue in Weekapaug which is just west of Quonochontaug. I also knew that if I got to Wequetequock ("Place Where It All Began") over in that place called Connecticut, I had gone too far. I also knew I lived in Washington County, the largest county in Rhode Island. (Did you know it is also the smallest largest county in the country?)

Of course this should come as no surprise since some of us actually know that Rhode Island is the smallest state in the country. I had been in RI just a few months but I had already learned that Rhode Island is about the size of a good forest fire, an average Texas ranch, and, as scientists recently determined, Rhode Island could fit quite nicely on a big piece of Antarctica that's now headed for the tropics.

So, at 563 square miles, how could I miss Washington County? I kept heading east and found myself in a maze of McMansions. Keep in mind, this was before the ubiquitous wannabe hardware store Benny's and former Benny's were plentiful enough to become land-based beacons for those of us who otherwise tried our best to stay safely south of the Slocum Grange and endless turf fields.

Yeah, yeah! I have asked for directions in Rhode Island in the past. Folks didn't exactly lie to me but I do think they made stuff up. I don't know. I was well into my second six pack by then. If I asked for clarification like "yeah but, do I turn east or west off Boston Neck Road?" I got total silence.

It was the longest thirty miles of my life. Down past Conimicut Point, dead end, back up, head towards Chepiwanoxet, then on to Appenaug, Quidnessett, Quonset, another dead end, back up, head towards Cocumcussoc, Pettaquamscut, Wakamo, but, when I spotted Jerusalem from Galilee, I said to myself, Jesus! This can't be Israel! And I was right!

I asked for directions in Milt's, a bar packed with large friendly men wearing flannel shirts and smelling of cannabis, boiler makers, and dead fish. There I learned that Galilee is really an Algonquin name for "Place of Staggering White Men." So, once more, dead end, back up, head toward Wenannatoke and the bountiful Richard P. Baccari Burial Ground and Shopping Mall. This is the Native American Burial Ground located right behind the Narragansett Mall. From there, go west, into the sunset, towards Matunuck and Ninigret, onward to home.

Now you may say getting lost was all my fault. Maybe it was the beer, or my inability to pronounce Cocumcussoc outloud. Besides, there are still a lot of empty Benny's left so what's my problem? Well, let me tell you what my problem is. I believe our leaders are complicit in a conspiracy to keep us running in circles and wandering directionless.

Let's take a look at one organization that claims to bring us peace and prosperity if only we vote the way they tell us to and buy all their stuff. I'm talking about the organization that calls itself the Southern Rhode Island Chamber of Commerce. Their mission is to "…advance the commercial, financial, industrial and civic interests of the community." It goes on to say "It is the one device that brings together the business and professional interests of the community, permitting them to accomplish collectively what none of them could do individually."

Damn right! No individual, not even Donald Trump, could get us so lost. For example, look at their name. The Chambers of Commerce in Narragansett, Charlestown, Westerly and North Kingstown did look and brought suit. They said "Really! We're in southern Rhode Island too. What's up with that?"

Now I can understand that the formerly named South Kingstown Chamber of Commerce could stand on Pettaquamscut rock, look out over Narrow River and fail to see a town, fail to see the hallowed "Main

Street" that is essential to the very existence of these "Main Streeters." Sure, from Pettaquamscut you can see lawyers escaping from northern Rhode Island, dogs defecating while dragging their so called masters down a pretty crescent beach, and students passed out on lawns. But, in Narragansett, there's no there there.

And, try finding Charlestown's main street from the balcony of one of those hideous beach houses in Green Hill. Talk about Mini Super! Charlestown doesn't even have its own high school for God's sake. A recent NECAP (New England Common Assessment Program) test showed that 47% of the kids from Hopkinton don't know how to spell CHARIHO and only 35% of their parents could locate it on a map.

And Westerly, westerly of what, I ask? Do you know where to get your mail if you live in Pawcatuck, Connecticut? You need to paddle over to the east bank of the mighty Pawcatuck and get your mail in … yes, Westerly. So, despite the Misquamicut Purchase over 300 years ago, even the Federal Government isn't so sure where Westerly is either. And given Westerly's history, it's no big surprise that Misquamicut is an Algonquin expression meaning "What Cheer? My Ass!"

And, did you know that seventy-two percent of Rhode Islanders think Westerly is in Connecticut and, get this, twenty three percent of the folks living in Westerly think they live in Connecticut. As for North Kingstown, all I see from the 245 ft. top of Yawgoo Valley Ski Area is endless turf farms, pumpkin patches and hemp (yes hemp). Maybe the North Kingstown Chamber of Commerce should rebrand itself "The Northern Rhode Island Chamber of Commerce."

Maybe Judge Stern was right in finding that The South Kingstown Chamber of Commerce was really The Southern Rhode Island Chamber of Commerce, but rumor has it, he lives in Little Compton and is afraid of bridges.

MOONSTONE BEACH

Many millions of years ago molten rock pushed from deep in the earth to form mountains in the north. Eons later it turned cold and started to snow. Snow fell season after season until the mountains were covered by mile-high glaciers. As the glaciers grew and spread they started to slide south, inch by inch, foot by foot, mile by mile. They carried the mountain tops along on their slow journey to the south. When warmer weather stopped the march of the glaciers, boulders and rocks from the mountain tops were spread throughout the land. Some made it to the ocean. Fierce storms and endless tides broke and polished them to smooth round stones, moonstones.

12,000 years ago, as the last of the glaciers retreated from Rhode Island, life returned. As the sea rose, early humans pushed north to what was once called Rhode Island & Providence Plantations, now simply Rhode Island. The boundary between sea and land provided a bountiful menu, some of which the reader may know as surf & turf, calamari, stuffies, whole bellies and one pound chix. The list is long. For millennia the sea also provided seaweed and a bottom feeding crustacean called lobster to nurture the three sisters (squash, corn, and beans) known today as heirloom veggies. In recent years, triggered by the advent of the five day work week and the Model A Ford, a trickle of people soon grew to a flood of summer pilgrims, all making their way to this boundary between land and sea in order to lay prone in the sun and work on their tans. Some dermatologists may also refer to this as "paying off my Lamborghini."

The rapid rise in the importance of a good tan has not gone without its problems. The obvious one is falling asleep or passing out in the noonday sun with only the nostalgic smell of Noxzema to mitigate the pain, blisters, and peeling skin—although for some, peeling skin can be of interest if not outright fun. Another more pervasive problem is the tan line. Although a recent Governor snuck off to Argentina to admire the tan lines of his "soulmate" (his words), it may be said in all fairness that he was from South Carolina, where loony is a prerequisite for political office. In fact, he got reelected before the soulmate's tan lines even faded. Nevertheless, besides porn stars, an amazing number of highly moral people are deeply concerned about their tan lines.

What to do? One answer is the tanning booth. I have never been to a tanning booth, so dear reader, you are free to ignore or disbelieve any of the following. Let me just say, I will never let one of my daughters go to a tanning salon. Because, if she went, I fear I would never see her again except as a full body image posted on Twitter. Another option is skin creams but who wants their daughter to look like she spent time with Donald Trump. This brings us to the heavenly days of Moonstone—the days before the Piping Plover wars. Moonstone Beach is a beautiful strand of sand in Southern Rhode Island fronting Block Island Sound, otherwise known as the Atlantic Ocean. Moonstone was a nude beach. If asked, I imagine many folks at Moonstone would say and might even believe that they were there to work on their tan lines. They might also claim to prefer Moonstone because wet bathing suits suck. Especially on those cool clear late August days when it seems you can reach out and touch Block Island. Others might claim they are there for those terrific coed volleyball games or one-on-one paddle ball.

At its height Moonstone was a carnival, a carnal carnival to be sure, but also a carnival of people, a carnival of nature. The beach was clean even though there was no town, state, or federal cleanup crew. Most folks took out their own trash, and there were enough do-gooders around to pick up for slobs who didn't. Moonstone was a magical moment in time.

On a high summer Sunday, a New Yorker parks right in front of a cop writing parking tickets. To them the fine is just another beach fee. A Darwinian selection process is at play. Just about everyone is fit and beautiful, and, those who aren't don't seem to care. A wiry gymnast cartwheels almost the length of the beach; a musician composes on his keyboard, takes his tenor sax to the water's edge and plays sweet melancholy; the bloodshot always-tipsy guy makes a gorgeous sand mermaid being devoured at the water's edge by a misogynist sand alligator; phantasmal sand castles and statues stand guard at the water's edge. The classy first-time fiftyish woman deftly unhooks the straps on her bathing suit top and discreetly lays on her belly. By the end of the day she's frolicking in the surf naked but still classy; the stylish paddleball girl wears a fine gold chain on her hips; the shapely woman well into her pregnancy. Wow! That's my wife! Yet another magical moment.

A Winter's Day

Shame Us the dog climbs a tree. Circa 1972.

Today, I'm feeling pretty good. A wonderful storm passed through late last night leaving silence under a thick blanket of white. Silence broken only by the occasional plow scraping snow in the dead of night. I have been waiting for this since Thanksgiving, but now, all is well. We're well past the solstice. The sun is beginning to awaken, and January 25 is, on average, the coldest day of the year. So, now the days will linger and the snow may stay a while. My fellow XC ski partners will soon be here. Weekdays, they work and I ski alone. I figure if anything happens, it might take a while to find me, but I should be well-preserved.

Today we will go to Arcadia. The Great Swamp is only ten minutes away but Arcadia is worth the extra twenty minutes. The storm pulled in that cold clear Canadian air. Still a bit blustery but at Arcadia we'll mostly stay in the woods out of the wind. Besides, Breakheart Pond is always a beautiful place to start from.

For those of you who only have one leg or one lung, I want you to know this is not about skiing. Just as kayaking is not about paddling (at least not for me), this piece is about making your way to a place of magic, be it a rocky shore or a snow-hushed woodland. This fine winter day is as good as it gets. And, you get it without the mosquitos, deer ticks, poison ivy, pollen, mud, or rain.

Snow offers a wonderland that has been amply described by many others, but you must experience it firsthand to begin to appreciate it in all its subtle, awe-inspiring majesty. Even a high-def CYAN screen can't fully capture the clear blue sky that has rolled all the way down from Canada to lift your spirits. You can't click your remote to the ginger crystals spreading before you as the sun slowly eases its way to nightfall. I wonder if nature removes its foliage so we can see further, see more of its beauty, think more clearly.

Jack working on his winter tan.
Circa 1972.

Have you ever seen a rainbow when a playful zephyr blows new snow from a pine bough? Have you seen blue shadows in a field of white, sublime curves sculpted by wind, water suspended in mid-air, bushes transformed to crystal chandeliers, a pond filled with diamonds?

The beauty of winter is visceral. If you ever tasted snowflakes, felt them melt on your face, made angels in the snow, threw a snowball, made a snowman, licked an icicle when you were young, but now feel the kiss of winter only when dashing between home and car, I advise you to head to the nearest woodland on a fine winter's day.

The winter forest offers more than beauty. Tracks stitch the snow, etching a calligraphy of motion and life. From deer to mice, from hawks to finches, we see where they have been, where they were headed, what they have done. Sometimes we see drama, life and death stories. Once I saw two fan-like imprints in the snow, imprints of large wings, maybe a red tail hawk, surrounding several small critter tracks and a few drops of blood.

I lied about the skiing part. If you can do it, it's the best way to go. In 1972, I attended a free workshop in Hanover, New Hampshire given by XC Ski Hall of Famer, John Caldwell. That morning, I learned all I needed to get out and enjoy. This included poling, camber, waxing, etc. But the best advice came when John asked "How many Catholics here?" Now, I once was an altar boy but surrounded by a bunch of Ivy League, Nordic-type Dartmouth folks I didn't raise my working class Catholic hand. John then said something that has served me all these years: "Think genuflect!"

What he was telling us was to put our whole body into it. All else will follow. That was great advice on many levels. It's all you really have to know to enjoy the pleasure of the winter woodland while waltzing through it, the only sound the music in your head and the rhythmic whisper of your skis. It's even good for you. As my cardiologist says, "If it doesn't kill you, it's good for you."

Yes! I'm feeling pretty good!

10

MUSIC, OFF KEY AND ON

Jack - "Music, a part of my life."
Circa 2013.

MY PLAYLIST

I confess, visual arts often leave me with feet aching and eyes glazed, but music is part of my life, part of me. Although I have a voice that has been likened to goose farts on a muggy day, music still makes me want to sing, dance, twist and shout, snap my fingers, clap my hands, tap my feet. Music can make me laugh; it can make me cry. It makes strangers friends, lovers love, tribes bond, movies better. It helps armies march. It keeps us awake in church. We get married, graduate, and are buried to music.

These days, music on our smart phones helps define who we are. We know our playlist is way more sparkling than our parents' lame stuff and so much more elegant than our children's heavy metal bombast. But I know better than to try to lay my playlist on you, 'cause you know yours is way better than mine. And, what about your playlist of life's milestones? Some of mine are:

The Clancy Brothers "Will ye go, Lassie go" at my mother's funeral; Leonard Bernstein conducting Samuel Barber's Adagio For Strings at Bobby Kennedy's funeral; taps as another veteran can't dodge the final salvo of time; a solo sax playing a measured Amazing Grace at a friend's funeral; the entire church singing it through bitter tears at another; buying my first record—The Ramparts' "The Death of Emmet Till" about a 14 year old black boy from Chicago murdered in Mississippi for allegedly flirting with a white woman. I was 14 then too; the look on my son's face when I showed him the simple three chord progression he needed to play most of his favorite Top Ten Hits; Black kids in the project bongo drumming to "My Bonnie Lies Over the Ocean." That's right. "My Bonnie Lies Over the Ocean." Music is indeed universal— from the young man singing a Gaelic lament in an Irish bar, to black and white kids singing Doo-wap songs in the Connecticut Valley and White and Black kids singing Doo-wop songs in the fields, beating out rhythms on the sides of the bus taking us home; The Kingsmen's garage band classic "Louie Louie" as we drive through primordial Louisiana swampland looking for the Mardi Gras; the sexual smoke of Bo Diddley's electric blues at an Alan Freed "Rock & Roll Review"; The crisp clean riffs off Jim Hall's jazz guitar; the sweet melancholy of Paul Desmond's sax; John Coltrane's turning the cute "My Favorite Things" into a jazz classic; "Home Cookin'" on Jimmy Smith's Hammond B3 organ; the baroque counterpoint of Nina Simone's jazz piano; the haunting simplicity of Eric Satie's piano pieces.

Yes! Music is part of me. As the Violent Femmes sing, I love American Music and then some. The list is endless. Enjoy!

Living Cheryl Wheeler's "Quarter Moon"

"And they seem to know each other very well
They speak across the garden and not a soul could tell
They can read the summer sky
and they can hear the back brook swell
And they seem to know each other very well"

The DePalmas. Circa 1968.

These are lyrics to the Cheryl Wheeler song "Quarter Moon." I love that song. It brings back a time when I bought my first house and found I bought more than a house; but then, I always have been lucky. Lucky to buy my first house from two old timers who lived that song even though they never heard it. Back then, I barely heard it. But, over the years, Angelo and Florence DePalma became my everyday heroes. Together they told me where I wanted to go, who I wanted to be, what was important, how to do things right. And, they did this without saying a word.

"She brings me plants and flowers all the time
And we dig the holes together she has to help with mine
When she pats the soil around them
oh my god, her eyes can shine
She brings me plants and flowers all the time

In 1968 I bought an early 1800s ten room farmhouse on 80 acres in Plainfield, NH. I bought it from Angelo DePalma for $15,000. I didn't have the $2,000 for a down payment but Dartmouth College used some of its hefty endowment to provide mortgages to employees who didn't have a down payment handy. It was the boost into the home-owning middle class that I needed. The property included a post and beam barn with a shed attached that had once been a blacksmith shop. Hand lettering on the shed door said "10 miles 88 rods to Lebanon Town Hall.

The treasure in that barn included a fully-equipped 1953 Farmall Cub tractor; an antique ice box; a lifetime of tools, nuts, bolts, lumber; all kinds of railroad stuff; and a pile of unused left-handed work gloves. We agreed to the sale on a handshake. When we closed, Angelo had to buy a padlock for the kitchen door so he could give me a key to the house. There wasn't a lawyer or real estate agent in sight. Angelo and his wife Florence moved to a house they had built for themselves across the road and over the years they proved to be good neighbors, wonderful friends, and powerful role models. Years after Angelo died I got word that Florence passed the night before. I worried about how my mother, who was also well along in years, would take the news. "How did she die?" "Ma, they tell me she just went to sleep." A pause. … "She always did things right."

"And they drive up north on Sunday afternoons
And he buys her wooden windmills
and she knows them by their tunes
And they drive up north on Sunday afternoons"

Angelo grew up in Revere, MA. In the early thirties he was working for the B&M Railroad in the White River Jct. switching yard when he slipped under a train and lost his left arm and some toes. He was taken to Mary Hitchcock Hospital in Hanover, NH where Florence, his nurse and future wife, took good care of him. B&M Railroad gave Angelo $1,200 and promised a job for life. Angelo and Florence married, bought the farm, and raised two kids. He learned to pitch hay with one arm. I learned a lot being around them in their winding-down years: how to live, how to die, how to do things right.

> *"And they speak about their lives as almost gone*
> *Waiting for the sunset from an old and distant dawn*
> *Selling off the land except the part they're living on*
> *And they speak about their lives as almost gone"*

They have been gone longer now than all the years I knew them. But they are still a big part of my life. I want to live like them, be like them still. And, I am better for it. Thank you Cheryl.

11

QUESTS

Wandering Jack finds a friend.
2008.

Elephanta Island (also called Gharapuri Island or Place of Caves) is less than an hour's ferry ride from Mumbai's Gateway of India. It is a popular tourist destination with interesting temples built into caves. It offers a nice break from the chaos of Mumbai. As with many things in India there are far more sellers than buyers and meager infrastructure. In Elephanta, this means more ferries than docking spaces. And, as with many things in India, folks don't let those minor details get in their way. As each ferry arrives, it simply ties up to the ferry before it. This results in a string of ferries tied belly to belly happily bobbing up and down in choppy Mumbai harbor. Passengers then jump from boat to boat hoping they are not going down when the boat is coming up. One slip and there would be few complete bones left to burn. There was an old woman on my boat well over ninety years and not much over ninety pounds who was tossed from boat to boat until she was set down on the dock looking about as excited as a senior citizen entering Walmart. Clearly Darwin is hard at work here. There may be a few more missing limbs and untimely deaths but those who make it are far more nimble than folks you might bump into at the mall.

How did we ever create this nimble gap? Take a look at how we protect our kids. Kids in the US just know that all traffic stops when the school bus stops. It's a law of nature just as certain as the falling apple. An Indian kid would be dumbstruck at the notion of a bus made just to carry him to school. If he observed a middle aged lady repeatedly lumbering off the bus and bowing at the wheels he might reasonably conclude that this was some kind of Indian religious ritual, like the Hindu ringing a bell when entering the temple.

He would not comprehend the time, energy, and money we spend to ensure that our children's lives are free of pain, disappointment, and danger. Crossing guards, pick up lists, seat belts, coaches, assistant coaches, nannies, nanny coaches, engaged parents, parent coaches, zero tolerance, schedules, IEPs, 504s, Ritalin—the list grows with each new threat, with each disturbing report at eleven. Unfortunately, all too often this means lives devoid of adventure, surprise, and yes, danger. A sad casualty in our earnest attempt to create a Novocaine nirvana for our kids is the quest.

The quest was more important to the development of my character than any school, sports team, Boy Scout troop, church, guidance counselor, or probation officer. It was scary, fun, and 100% ADULT-FREE. We had to make our own judgments, our own decisions. Do we go through or around enemy territory, attack or retreat, take it or break it, kill it or feed it, stick it out or quit, vote on it or fight over it? Leadership ranged from monarchy to anarchy but somehow, we figured it out. Quests ran the gamut from cutting through enemy territory on the walk home from school to the ultimate in questing—The Great Escape.

THE GREAT ESCAPE

Every kid I knew including me wanted to run away from home. Some of us some of the time, others most of the time. This yearning kicked in well before we read about Tom or Huck. It was instinctive. Kids ran away all the time for all your standard reasons, but, when enough "most of the time" kids reached a critical mass the plan begins to look better and better to the "sometime kids" and a legendary great escape was in the works.

I was too young to do the last one in my neighborhood. Jimmy McDonald and Johnny Smith headed it up. Jimmy was smart. Johnny was not but looked like a grown man. To be legendary you had to have a lot of kids—eight kids from five families took off. You had to get far away—they got to New Jersey from Hartford, Connecticut. It had to be at least overnight–gone for five days. It had to include freights–New York, New Haven & Hartford RR. It had to involve police–several times. It also helped if the outcome included some time in reform school or a good beating, preferably public, when they got home–yes to both. The best thing was the stories. The stories became legends. No one had proof other than what the returnees would tell us. Did Johnny really pull a forty-five on a railroad cop? Did the kids really go in one door of a New Jersey State Police car, out the other side and get away? We believed what we wanted to and we wanted to believe it all. That's what legends are for. History thrives on quests. It's in our DNA. Nowadays I'm happy to see many young people who can afford it traveling to exotic places all over the globe. It will be good for them and good for their children. And when they do have children I hope they understand the quest begins at home.

KENNY

I knew him for about half an hour. His name was Kenny Hanson— nineteen years old. He had those rosy cheeked outdoor good looks most fathers would be proud of—and a complexion most mothers would envy. He wore an oversize hooded winter parka that had a vague chainsaw aroma, baggy non-nondescript jogging pants, ratty red sneakers, and one of those Tibet-style knitted toques that brings to mind young middle class dreadlocked males kicking Hacky Sacks around.

My son Brendan picked Kenny up hitchhiking in Providence. My wife Gerry and I learned of his presence when we came back from our Sunday walk on the beach and were told a hitchhiker was in the shower and his dog, Lucifer, a pit bull who occasionally bit people, was in our van. You might say my guard was up.

After the shower, Brendan cooked Kenny up some leftovers. In the following half hour or so we talked. He was raised in Missoula, Montana, has five brothers and one sister—"half sister really." The brothers live with their various birth fathers. Kenny left his father when he was fourteen. They did not get along. The brothers were taken from his mother because she had been into drugs and alcohol. Kenny told us "She had a few DUIs and stuff like that but nothing real bad. She joined the military to get straight and is clean now." The six- or eight-year-old sister (he's not sure which age) lives with his mother in a town near Richmond, Virginia—he's not sure which town but he's headed to Virginia anyway.

About a year ago he left Missoula to live in Presque Isle, Maine. I don't know why he left Missoula or who he stayed with in Presque Isle, but he left there about a month ago to visit the sister he has never seen.

Given a shabbily dressed six footer with a pit bull hitching rides in northern New England, it is not surprising it took him a month to get to Rhode Island from Maine. Brendan was only his third ride so far since he started out. He tries to stay on secondary roads like Route 1 because he'll get busted or fined hitching the interstates. He has no maps. He walks at least twenty miles a day. He spent a few days in Boston and took in about $90 a day standing in Harvard Square with his dog Lucifer and a sign. He left because he was afraid he would lose his dog. He couldn't afford to comply with Massachusetts pit bull laws. He sleeps outside most of the time. He has one blanket with him.

What struck me was the incongruity of it all. Here's a kid in a hard situation who goes on a questionable quest and brings a pit bull along. He's crazy right? Crazy and probably dangerous. But, if you were in my kitchen on that Sunday I bet you would say to yourself "what a nice young man."

When Kenny started to leave, Gerry made up a little bag of food and followed me into the bedroom. We both had the same idea. I laid my twenty on hers. We both laughed. I wished him luck. Gerry hugged him and slipped him the two twenties. His mouth opened but no words came out. Brendan drove him out to the highway. Later we all were sorry we didn't ask him to stay. I know! I know! He could be a serial killer, a petty thief, or an opportunistic con man. The best I can figure is Kenny needs someone to take care of—be it his dog, his sister, his mother. Who knows? What I don't know is who's going to take care of Kenny?

12

HERE & THERE

I never had a mentor—at least not your standard wise and worldly grandfather type. I could have used one. I had to figure things out for myself—almost always the hard way. I was a product of a single parent family before Single-Parent became a condition. It never occurred to me to ask anyone for advice about life's big decisions. In fact, I really didn't know there were decisions to be made, didn't know I had choices. So instead of mentors, I found role models.

Most of them would be shocked to learn that I considered them role models. Not one of them was perfect. In fact, they all had flaws, some of them major, but as I got to know them, they inspired some part of me that needed inspiring. None of this was planned. It was mostly subconscious and became clear to me only in hindsight. In my long career I was lucky to have almost all good bosses. I know folks who seem to have only bad bosses. My bosses helped make me a better worker, boss, father, and husband. Is there a lesson here? Here is a story on one of my role models.

A DIAMOND IN THE ROUGH

I learned a lot from a boss who never seemed to be teaching. He was Rick Petrocelli, VP for Business and Finance at the University of Rhode Island. He surely didn't look like a university executive. In fact, he made Danny DeVito look like Arnold Schwarzenegger. And yes, Rick even grew up on Federal Hill, the son of immigrants. Some of his boyhood friends grew up to be important legislators or important crooks, sometimes both.

When he walked into a room you might take him for the caterer at best. He made that trait his strength. He paid attention and gave you respect whoever you were. So, when he started talking, he had your attention, had your respect. On Federal Hill he earned a Ph.D. in the chemistry of life. He went on to earn another Ph.D. in chemistry, this one from Providence College. He headed a company that made batteries for submarines. He was the first RI Commissioner of Higher Education. He founded the RI Children's Crusade that provides scholarships for disadvantaged children who stayed in school. He got things done.

He knew about power. He knew about leadership. The thing was, he did it his way. He was the same person, whether with the governor or with a janitor. He didn't waste any energy putting on a work face. He bragged to us whenever he bought a tie that cost less than a buck. He seldom spent time at his staff meetings checking on our projects. Instead, he brought the outside world back to us, helped us see that we were part of a larger picture. He used to tell me, "John, if I get to know a lot about your job, you're in trouble. Just tell me what you need to get the job done."

He always had a colorful way to make a point. He once told us that believing is the best revenge. Then explained, "When someone comes into my office to complain about some incompetent, evil coworker, I ask for the bad guy's phone number and pick up the phone. The complainer almost always asks me, "What are you doing?"

"I'm going to fire the SOB. Oh! No! No! No! Don't do that!"

Once when we were dealing with a tough problem, someone suggested we bring the University lawyer in. Rick responded "We got lawyers to keep us out of jail, not to tell us how to run the damn place. First, figure out what you want to do, then call the lawyer." He once sent his management team at the battery company he headed to the first *Godfather* film to study its management principles.

So what did I learn from this boss?

- Always be yourself.
- Make your weakness your strength.
- And my corollary: Don't let your strength become your weakness.
- Study people and human nature.
- Remember who's in charge and who has a stake.
- Start with respect.
- Don't micromanage.
- Paint the big picture.
- Get it done.

STILL WARM

So what the hell am I doing standing by the edge of the road holding this guy's hand? My heart's going like a jackhammer. My whole body's going like a jackhammer. It's no use. My pulse is his pulse. I can't tell. His hand is warm! Damn! It almost feels hot! Is that my sweat? Did he just move? I'm shaking. In a way I hope he's dead because I don't know what the hell to do next. Weird! So quiet. Dreamy ground fog, persistent peepers somehow adding to the silence. White pine and poplar saplings quietly winning their battle for the meadow.

Where are the sirens and flashing lights? The ambulance? The red Mustang's about two feet off the ground wrapped around a big elm. His arm dangles out the window like a girl drying her hair. The pulse bit ain't working. I let his hand go. Still warm. "Hey man! You okay?" I sound so stupid I laugh. But the sound of my voice challenges the silence. Challenges the weirdness.

Screw this! What's next on the agenda? I want to do right. I lift his arm gently back through the window and pull on the door handle. The weight of the arm surprises. The sprung door creaks and shrieks but opens with alarming ease. I mean what if I have to give artificial respiration? Where the hell is everyone! The guy is still in the driver's seat. But the driver's seat is pushing this poor bastard's chest deep into the steering wheel. I feel shame that I feel relief that there is nothing I can do. He'll need a Jaws of Life to get him out of there.

I didn't stop when I first saw the car wrapped around the tree. I didn't stop until I ran over the windshield lying in the road. All this craziness took time to register. It was so quiet, so country road normal, so casual. The driver behind me stops only because I did. He would have gone around me but my open car door blocked the way. He took one look and announced he would go for help. I'm vaguely pissed he's leaving me here alone but this is before cell phones so it makes sense. He just didn't leave any room for me to decide I would be the one to go for help. It's been at least twenty minutes and still no help and I'm trying to figure out the right thing to do when there is nothing I can do. I know I can't just leave this guy. I pull the windshield off the road. There are fresh skid marks. Two sets side by side. One turning toward the tree.

Finally a car comes along. I flag it down. Great! But it's not a cop. It's a middle aged couple. I figure they're dating not married—at least not to each other. They obviously have been drinking and the woman has a loud mouth. I start to explain but with a few wobbly steps she waves me off and heads to the car. "I'm a nurse. Let me through." She walks up to the car and reaches in. "Oh! He's dead alright. Look at his stomach. Hard as a rock. Filled with blood." For some reason I resent her remarks. Like she didn't have the right to talk about him—to be the one to pronounce him broken, pronounce him dead. "Let's get out of here honey. The cops back there are going to be all over this goddam place."

The cops finally do come, take my name and say I can leave. I read about the crash in *The Lebanon Valley News* the next day. The young man who died that night had recently returned from Vietnam and now lived about twenty miles south in Claremont. It took the cops all that time to get to the scene of his death because they were investigating an accident about a half mile back. Two cars were reported to be racing/chasing each other and one of them knocked down some guard rails on a turn. When the police got the second call they thought they were already at the scene. The racing cars were never identified.

The car stripped a good sized piece of bark off that elm, but the tree seemed to thrive anyway. Before long, the scar turned a weathered gravestone grey. I often return to New Hampshire to camp and take care of some land I still own. Last year, heading into town, I saw the tree was gone and the hay meadow a lush green. White pine and poplar saplings mowed clean, quietly waiting still for another round.

AN AMERICAN SATURDAY MORNING

It's Saturday. My buddy Dennis and I drive 45 minutes to get to Vinny's Barbershop in Coventry, Rhode Island. On these first come first serve Saturdays we have to wait a while more, but I actually look forward to reading from Vinny's magazines while waiting. Besides all the standards like *Sports Illustrated, Time,* the daily newspaper etc., I can read about how Napoleon was loved by his troops in *Military History* or read about how to provide your weekend guests with a hefty dose of Southern hospitality in *Garden & Gun*. It's sort of like Martha Stewart meets Robert E. Lee. Besides the magazines, Vinny has a TV always tuned to European soccer games. It's great for folks who want to brush up on their Italian.

Vinny's Barbershop supports three barbers and three generations. There is a division of labor based on the age of the customers. A warm, friendly woman does a great job with the squirmy sticky crowd brought in by their proud moms and pops. The young barber wearing a Patriots #12 hoodie and a backward Red Sox greets his tattooed clients with a fist bump. And Vinny delivers the best haircut to guys with the least hair, at least the least hair where they want it to be.

Here's what you get: he'll wash your hair if needed; he'll cut your hair with scissors and trim it with several electric razors; he'll trim your beard; he'll cut your hair in all the places it's not supposed to be. Yes, all the places. He'll shave you with a straight razor and top it off with a bracing aftershave and in the cold of winter you can knock back a holiday shot to warm your insides. All this back then for twenty bucks.

There is always a waiting line for Vinny. It's mostly older guys and I suspect they don't come and wait just for the magazines or the top shelf treatment or even the price. I think they also come because they have been around long enough to recognize quality, to value a real professional. A professional who, haircut after haircut, day after day always delivers his best as if best all the time is normal, as if standing on his feet all day is a walk in the park, as if he can't imagine doing it any other way.

When Vinny came to this country he was 15 years old. He wore tight bell bottoms with no pockets. He talked funny. We need more Vinnys. We need them bad.

A guy comes in and greets Vinny like he's his favorite uncle. Vinny tells him there's three guys ahead of him.

"Vinny, you know I'll wait." Then turns to us and says "Yeah, just got back home from Gulfport, Mississippi yesterday. Drove over here from Putnam, Connecticut. Vinny knows I'll wait. He's the only barber that ever touched my hair. He's the best. Am I right?"

The guys waiting nod like they're in church while this Putnam guy starts a one way conversation. He looks to be in his forties, heavy but fire plug solid, wiry salt and pepper hair standing straight up like he just woke up from a quick nap in the electric chair. Energy just jumping off him.

"Man my dog missed me. Stayed up all night waiting by the window. Just knew I was 'a comin' home to Daddy! I had the balls ready. The dog not the wife. Man! This dog is smart. She got four balls. No I mean it—red white blue and yellow. I tell her to get the red ball. It's the red ball she gets. She'll go all day."

A customer asks, "How'd ya like it?"

"Mississippi or my wife?"

Polite chuckles.

"It's okay. The money's good and I'm renting a house 4 bedrooms, big garage, swimming pool, hot tub, the whole works for 800 bucks and in the good part of town too. Know what I mean?"

"Yeah, I know. Man you're not gonna find deals like that around here. Would you like to live in Mississippi?"

"No way! Ya know I'm always looking for good workers. I'm in demolition. Good money. I'm demolishing a strip mall the size of two football fields, right next to the police station so there's still a lot of copper and other salvage stuff left over—all gravy. I ship it all over the world to get the best price. Made $14,000 bucks last shipment. I pay my guys real good too but I can't find no workers. They're all still collecting from Katrina. Trailers falling apart. No one wants to work down there. Know what I mean?"

"Last week I'm in a parking lot and a guy walks up behind me and puts a big ass knife right on my Adam's apple. I say 'Hey buddy I'll give you my wallet just don't hurt me ok?' I don't give him time to say yes or no. I reach into my jacket pocket and point the barrel of my big ass Glock over my shoulder. All that asshole can see is a 45 cal barrel pointing right at his little ass. I says 'Okay buddy, you have two choices. You can lay on the ground on your belly or you can lay on the ground on your back. Your choice.' You know what the cop says when he finally gets there? 'You shoulda shot the son of a bitch. You had every legal right to nail him.'"

"So, nah! I don't want to live there. Besides it's 90 degrees at 7am and over 100 by noon. I fly up here every month, Friday to Tuesday and spend the weekend with my dog—my wife too."

"Sounds pretty rough down there. Ever think of retiring?"

"Hell no! I'm having too much fun."

OUR TRIP AROUND THE USA—ALMOST

Prologue:

By the time I retired I had already seen quite a bit of this country, hitchhiking, canoeing, camping with family and friends. This trip included Gerry, my adventurous wife and savior, daughters Diamond, 13 years old, and Lizzie, 11. My son James did not actually go with us, but his exploits coming and going to and from Antarctica are part of the story. This trip was going to be different. We still looked forward to exploring the nooks and crannies of this great country and meeting its nook and cranny folks. What would make this trip special was the absence of deadlines. We could stop for as long as we wanted. Only homesickness, a drought in my garden, and the price of gas could turn our Recreational Vehicle (RV) toward home. For the first time in my life, I would live the legendary endless summer.

Did I say RV? I didn't have one. Never thought I would own one. I remember reading Steinbeck's *Travels with Charley*. Talk about getting old! The man who fed us *The Grapes of Wrath,* poured us wine from *Cannery Row* and introduced us to the folks at *Tortilla Flat,* spent half of *Travels with Charley* writing about his camper.

It occurred to me that cross country hitchhiking and even tent camping might not be embraced by my wife Gerry and teenage daughters. I knew we needed a camper. The three things I knew were:

1. I didn't know anything about RVs;
2. I didn't want to spend much money;
3. I wanted one small enough to let me navigate the nooks and crannies mentioned earlier.

Two years of searching later I still didn't know much about RVs, still didn't want to spend much money, and still wanted a small one. Oh! One more thing. Gerry would have to like it. I found that out when I got excited about a gutted four wheel drive RV for $3,500. It had been used as a beach fishing camp and looked like something out of Mad Max, smelled fishy and had no lights. Gerry was not as excited.

We finally found Joe's 1993, 21 foot Gulf Stream with 21,000 miles on it for sale for $11,500. Everything looked brand new even under the hood. This was the rig for us! Steinbeck would have approved. I then played to my weakness. "Look Joe, I'm not even gonna test drive it. Is there anything wrong with this baby?" He thought for a minute then mentioned a small crack in the tub made by a relative he meant to repair—the tub not the relative. "That's all I can think of." I thought Joe was telling the truth. I still do. I had withdrawn the $11,500 asking price from the bank. "Joe, I believe you. I have ten thousand here in my hand. Bring the RV down to my house in Kingston and we'll close the deal today." Joe showed up about two hours later and accepted my $10,000 offer. We bought us a real Recreational Vehicle! After a couple of shakedown cruises to New Hampshire that fall. we brought the RV for a final oil change/checkup and set out on our grand adventure in early spring—first stop Florida!

The Trip

4/3/2011 - Sunday - Greetings from the Greencastle Pennsylvania Public Library. We had gotten off to a good start Sunday until we stopped at a rest stop on Interstate 81 south of Harrisburg, Pennsylvania. We heard a funny noise coming from the engine and asked a savvy looking truck driver what he thought it might be. He said he thought the fan was hitting something and it would probably be okay to drive it to the next town to find a garage.

4/6/2011 - Wednesday - I am writing this on Wednesday afternoon waiting for a new engine to be installed. I had the oil changed just before we left RI. Big mistake! The oil drain plug was put back wrong. Damn good engine too. The final cost, not including what the truck stop food is doing to our life expectancy, will be over $6,000. The good news is we are becoming part of John's family. John owns the E.L.M. Garage in Greencastle and is patriarch of a large mechanically inclined family. John displayed his true patriarchal wisdom by declining to install the engine. But he did have a grandson Travis who was more than willing. What a great country! Got to go! Will send another update if anything else of interest happens.

I didn't expect another interesting event so soon. Phyllis, John the patriarch's daughter and garage bookkeeper, invited our girls to Game Night at the local United Otterbein Brethren Church—a forerunner of today's United Methodist Church. This Greencastle branch was founded in 1797 by Christian Newcomer, an associate of William Otterbein. Yeah. I also wondered why it wasn't called the United **Newcomer** Brethren Church. Maybe Christian Newcomer didn't want to be known as a *Newcomer*.

At any rate Gerry was invited too, so I tagged along to be close to her if something bad happened ... to me. We found ourselves in an apologetics class where the topic was the Holy Trinity. There was a lot of good energy in the church, but I had trouble following the logic. By the way I forgot to mention that one of my hearing aids broke the day we left so if God called, I may have missed the call. But, it was nice to be among folk who were obviously smarter and more spiritual than I. It was also comforting to know that most of them also could not figure what the Holy Spirit really looked like or what he/she/it did.

4/7/2011 - Thursday – also on this day, I received the following email from my Jewish brother-in-law:

```
Jack, thanks for the news... I call the
Trinity "3 in 1 oil" - without the can — a
slippery concept!"
Yours, David
```

4/9/2011 - Saturday – After almost a week camped behind the E.L.M. Garage and riding bikes all over Greencastle, we decided to rent a car for the weekend – maybe go to Gettysburg if the weather held. The rental agency sent a van to bring us to the car rental office. A fiftyish overweight black man pulled up and started updating his trip log. He didn't look up or seem to know or care if we were there. Once we got rolling things changed.

As usual Gerry got quickly to the man's story. It's amazing how she gets people to open up. Yet, there's no secret formula. All she does is listen closely and ask good questions that show she really is listening.

Gerry started with, "Did you live here all your life?"

"No. From Brooklyn. Was in the Detective unit. Came here three years ago."

"Why come here?"

"Got shot five times by a thirteen-year-old kid. Partner got killed. So did the kid."

Surely a compelling story but what amazed me was this man's sad resignation when he talked about the kid who created this tragedy. "Kid's been on the street since he was six, no father, not much for a mother, the street was all he knew." The man could have been talking about a son who had a terminal untreatable illness. We arrived at the rental agency all too soon.

4/10/11 - Sunday - Travis, John's grandson, finished the repairs late Saturday night in spite of having strep throat. We settled up and got rolling Sunday Morning. It felt good to be on the road again. My anxiety tank was still full, so I looked forward to putting some miles behind me to burn off the feeling that something bad was about to happen ... again. Ten miles down the road we stopped to gas up. The last time we stopped was in New Jersey before the engine problem and the full service attendant had a lot of problems filling the tank. This time, it was much worse. Gas started bubbling up and spilling on the ground! I yelled to Gerry to get the kids out of the RV and ran into the store past a line of customers and yelled at the clerk that the gas would not shut off. The manager came out and pulled the gas nozzle out of the RV. Gas no longer came from the RV, but my RV continued to occasionally belch gas. So... the problem was mine! The manager had a good old boy accent so I figured he knew more about cars than I did. Wrong again! Most of his theories didn't seem to hold water (or gas).

I called Travis. Despite his strep throat and the fact that my problem was not related to the new engine, he said he would meet me back at the E.L.M. Garage. He did and said "Let's fill her up." The gas pump continued to burp and belch every time we tried to fill the tank so Travis rolled under the RV and asked for a knife. I got him a knife and a minute later gas started pouring out under the RV. I went into emergency mode quickly considering all the possibilities, including setting a match to that puddle of gas. At that moment it seemed pretty logical to me. But Travis rolled out, stood up and said let's give her a try! This time the pump was still a bit trigger happy but much better. Travis then asked me to turn the RV around to face the other direction. Now the pump acted like a normal well-behaved pump.

We filled up, immensely grateful for the privilege of buying 30 gallons of gas at $3.80/gallon. This was tempered a bit by the realization that every time I got gas on this 10,000 mile journey I was going to have to figure out what side of the ground ran uphill and what side ran down. Lucky I have a level with me.

Note: The gas pump problem and solution—The RV has a 2 or 3 inch gas filler line that goes from the access point in the rear to the tank about 8 feet away. It also has another garden hose sized vent line that goes from the tank to just below the access point. As gas fills the tank the displaced air goes out the vent line. If you are at a pump where the slope puts the tank uphill from the access point the gas will back up in the filler line and eventually back up into the vent line. What Travis did was pull the vent hose down to create a low point then punctured it to drain the gas that was in it.

Still 4/10/11 - Sunday - We thanked Travis profusely and once more were on our way. Life was good. At dusk, we pulled into a rest stop in West Virginia. When it was time to leave, the RV wouldn't start. That's right! It would not start. The good news was that I was a paid up member of the Good Sam Club. No, not Sam Walton. Although Sam Walton is omnipotent and omnipresent, I think "Good Sam" refers to the Good Samaritan in the Bible but, unlike that Good Samaritan, Good Sam also tows RVs. I admit I kept thinking about this morning's convenient puddle of gas option but that did not seem to be a very good option here. So, Gerry calls Travis while I dial the Good Sam Emergency Road Service number.

Travis doesn't answer so Gerry leaves a message with him. I get a message giving Good Sam's weekday office hours. Desperate, I dial the office number on the Good Sam card and after another member ID security check and nine option calling tree, punctuated with bad music, Selepha whispers in my ear "Good Sam Emergency Road Service. How may I help you today?" (That's right, Selepha. I had her spell it.) I'm ecstatic! I'm talking to a real person, a beautiful person with a beautiful name, a person who wants to help me today. But how? We need a tow, but to where? Travis is more than 100 miles back up the road. Gerry's phone rings. It's Travis. I ask Selepha to hold on while I talk to my family mechanic. She tells me to take my time. She will be there as long as it takes.

I'm hoping Travis has a helicopter and will bring his tool box along or maybe he has mechanically adept relatives down here in West Virginia. Instead he asks me how it sounds when I try to start it. Can I try it now so he can hear it. I roll down the window and put my phone as close to the engine as I can reach. The folks parked next to us begin to look nervous.

The engine starts right up! Travis says it may be the fuel filter (cheap) or fuel pump (in the tank – expensive) or catalytic converter (expensive). He thinks the engine failure is related to temperature and will start after it cools down. I am not sure if he is saying all this just to make sure we put many miles between him and us but we take his advice. I thank Selepha for her patience and warn her I may be back in touch. "Anytime, Mr. Barry."

So now we have an RV that we are afraid to turn off and which occasionally spits up gas if facing the wrong way at the pump. We put a few more miles on and turn into a Flying J truck stop for the night. We hope we'll be able to start the RV in the morning. Not surprisingly when it gets dark we find the 12V coach lights do not work so we eat trucker food with headlamps on. I feel like I'm going deeper into the mine.

4/11/2011 - Monday - The next morning, we all hold our breath while I turn the key. The RV starts right up. I even guess right as to the tilt at the pumps, so we fill the tank and are on our way. Destination is several hours and fill-ups away in New Bern, North Carolina where we plan to visit old friends. Our visit with them is a most enjoyable and much needed hiatus from the road. The showers are wonderful; the food great; but, best of all, are Rich and Sharon's thoughtful hospitality and renewed friendship.

4/12/2011 - Tuesday - I bring the RV to a mechanic Rich recommends. He replaces the fuel filter which is clogged. The bill—under fifty bucks. I want to hug everyone in the garage. We tour New Bern—a neat little place with statues of bears all over town—great statues made in Bern, Germany. You know? That's the value of travel. I want my kids to know that there is much more to this world than Rhode Island's Mr. Potato Head statues.

4/13/2011 - Wednesday - Back on the road we head to Interstate 95 and take a break at the South Carolina Welcome Center. The Welcome

Center is closed but the restrooms are open which is a good thing because the RV again DOES NOT START!

This time we're nestled between diesel trucks that keep their engines running all night. Worse yet, Gerry spots a No Overnight Camping sign. I figure if a cop comes along and throws us in jail we'd be ahead of the game. But the sign bothers Gerry so I find a night caretaker who reminds me of Willy Nelson and explain our plight. She says "Honey, you don't have a worry in the world." I so wanted to believe her. Of course the 12V coach lights still don't work so we resume our miner routine and eat in the semi-dark surrounded by snarling diesel engines, or as Garnet Rodgers calls them "Chinese dragons with a thousand lights."

4/14/11 - Thursday - The next morning, the RV starts right up again so I overcome my dread of being overcharged and drive to a Ford Dealership in Florence, SC. Gerry had called earlier to explain our situation and ask if they could check out the RV. The place is a Dickensian mishmash of large dirty and cluttered hangar-like sheds and random chain link fences. The lady in charge brings us to a surprisingly clean waiting room and tells us she'd be back to "collect" us within the hour. Half hour later she leads us back to the RV. The mechanic can't get the engine to fail and all the computer diagnostics look good. She charges us nothing and advises us to head to our Florida destination and not turn the engine off until we get there. I ask the mechanic if he would drive us down for $1,000. They think I'm joking. At 11pm that night we get to my sister Pat's house in Florida. I love Pat. I love Florida. I love electricity.

4/14/2011 to 4/26/2011 - For the next couple of weeks we relax and enjoy Pat's company and hospitality. Besides the beautiful local beaches and nifty pool and hot tub at the gated community we do other relaxing things like buying Pat's house (just in case I can't start the RV), getting my infected ears fixed, things like that. In Florida I figured it was safe to de-winterize the RV. This is mainly attaching a hose from the house and turning on all the faucets to flush antifreeze from the RV water lines. When I turn on the hose, water starts pouring from the back of the RV. I have visions of wet rugs and tropical mold. It turns out the guy I hired to winterize the RV didn't close a drain valve. No harm but it did get my heart pumping, which is no small thing in an over-50 gated community.

4/27/2011 - Wednesday - I make an appointment at the local Ford dealer to change the oil on the new engine, recharge the cab A/C coolant that was drained when the new engine was installed and check the engine to find out why it still fails to start even after replacing the fuel filter. The good news is that all the readings look good. The bad news is that the coolant required by this vintage A/C is no longer made. The main reason we bought the RV was to escape the cold rainy Rhode Island spring by heading to warmer climes. So now I have an RV that will be great in Alaska. On Monday I am going to the RV place to try to find out why we lose the 12 volt coach power when we most need it. Wish me luck. Oh! I forgot. My other hearing aid broke. Now I can't even hear myself whine!

5/1/2011 - Saturday - *Received email from my good friend Steve White. He says "I recently read that whining is just anger forced through a small hole..."*

The real good news is that our son James will be coming home from Antarctica a month early. Although "coming home" in James speak means stops in Mexico and Argentina, we decide to head back to Rhode Island during the next tornado lull.

5/2/201 - Monday - I went to the RV place and got mostly good news. We killed Osama and threw him in the ocean. My 12V electrical problem may be fixed and Ricky, the A/C guy across the street from the RV place, might be able to recharge my A/C coolant. Maybe I don't have to limit my RV travels to Hudson Bay and points north after all.

Although we loved every minute spent in southwest Florida despite its billing as "The Lightning Capital of the World," it's time to head home. Weather forecasts a few tornado-free days where we might zip up the East Coast without fear of landing in Oz. We decide to leave tomorrow and start loading the RV for our return trip. I plug the house line into the RV to charge the batteries. A while later Gerry hears a hum coming from the RV electric panel and the panel cover feels hot. Damn her! Always stirring things up. I call the RV place. Even though it's almost an hour before closing time I get an answering machine. I leave a message for RC the RV electricity guru to call. We continue to load the RV. No call.

5/4/2011 - Wednesday - I call the RV place early the next morning. The guy who can't add even with the help of a calculator but nevertheless does the billing answers. "Oh RC? He only works here on Mondays and Tuesdays." Of course today is WEDNESDAY! Gerry notices that RC did indeed leave a message on my phone and the phone number he left is different than the RV place's number. I just can't get over what a wonderful and smart wife I have.

I call the number. RC works the other three days at an RV place just a few miles north of Englewood and in fact is only a mile or so off our route home. "RC! I'll be there within the hour!" RC fixes the hum and hot electric panel. Everything seems to be in working order. "How much do I owe ya?" "Oh! forty will do." I slip him sixty. Still better than $400. We head north!

After several hours we stop at a rest stop near Ocala, FL. Once again it fails to start. Notice the calmness now? No caps, no exclamation points. We know the drill. We're seasoned bad RV veterans. It's about time for lunch anyway. After a leisurely lunch, the RV starts right up and we're on our way again.

Early in the afternoon we get a call from our son Brendan. James has been in a car accident in Mexico and is in the hospital for observation. He is "good." The car was going about 70 when the woman who was driving lost control trying to avoid a tractor trailer. The car flipped and rolled before landing right side up. James crawled out the window and walked away with some cuts and bruises, although it took a few months for all the glass to work its way out of his arm. The woman, who was pregnant was a bit more beat up, but it appears that she and the baby are okay. James is headed for Buenos Aires and will be home as planned in early June.

Returning from a stint in Antarctica, the prior year, James was in downtown Christchurch, New Zealand the morning of the earthquake there. I liked his latest email to us from Mexico: "I'm okay ... again." Of course this is not completely reassuring. We know that James's okay is not your average okay. When James was about thirteen Gerry went out for the afternoon and, as usual, called home before returning.

"Hi James. How is everything at home?"

"Good."

"Does anyone need anything?"

Pause. "Well Dad might need a ride home from the hospital."

"HOSPITAL?"

Another pause. "Well he went in an ambulance with Auntie Catherine." Elderly Aunt Catherine died that night. Her parting mantra throughout the night was, "But kiddo, these are supposed to be my golden years."

We stop at Crooked River State Park, Georgia just over the Florida line. It is the first time we camp since starting our camping trip over a month ago. The place isn't spectacular, but it is peaceful. Before we leave I see a Carolina wren fly in and out of the RV side compartment that stores the electric hookup cable. Curious bird! It reminds us of how much we love camping and how many wonderful opportunities were lost. But hey! We're lucky to have so much to lose.

5/5/2011 - Thursday - Later that day we stop at a lovely mansion/ tourist info center in South Carolina—a pocket park shaded by magnificent live oak trees—perfect for a picnic. We'll stay the hour so I turn off the engine and pull the cable out to hook up the generator for the microwave. The cable compartment is filled with Carolina wren nesting material. I picture those little birds chasing us all the way back to Rhode Island. This "picture" is interrupted by smoky exhaust coming from the generator. So, no microwave till we get home. Just another item on our to-do list.

The mansion is filled with Southern genteel kitsch. The men's room has several old timey tin posters like you see in Cracker Barrel. (Sure!

As if you've never been to Cracker Barrel!) Anyway, one sign you're not apt to see in Cracker Barrel says:

> ### *BEER!*
> ### *HELPING UGLY PEOPLE HAVE SEX SINCE 1882!*

It got me to thinking how I could better spend all this wasted time stuck in rest stops. No! Not the sex part! What I'm thinking is making more interesting posters for Cracker Barrel or maybe running a contest on Twitter.

Speaking of Cracker Barrel, that night we stay at the
!!!!! SOUTH OF THE BORDER RV PARK!!!!!

which is part of

!!!!! SOUTH OF THE BORDER EVERYTHING ELSE PARK!!!!!

Sure; Like you've never heard of
!!!!! SOUTH OF THE BORDER !!!!!

This is the authentic American experience. If Barack simply presented a receipt proving he and Michelle spent a night at **!!!!! SOUTH OF THE BORDER !!!!!** all those Birthers would probably want to make him an honorary Navy Seal. By the way, have you heard that the Disney Corporation has applied for a "Seal Team 6" trademark? And all this time I thought Donald Trump was largely responsible for the decline of Western Civilization.

Note! The comments on Birthers and Donald Trump were written in 2011. And the guy is still at it. God help us!

5/6/2011 - Friday - A thunderstorm and four jammed lanes of traffic in Northern Virginia convinces us to spend our last night on the road in a Wal*Mart parking lot. Plenty of lightning but no tornado, and there's a Chinese restaurant nearby.

5/7/2011 - Saturday - After paying $4.29/gal. in NY, we reluctantly stop for gas at an Interstate 95 Service Center ghetto west of New Haven, Connecticut. This place could rival Mogadishu for lack of organization, efficiency, and cleanliness. It must have been fatigue or a strong death wish. I inadvertently TURN THE ENGINE OFF. And I also can't get the gas station pump to work. After trying all combinations of credit cards, debit cards, PINS, and zip codes, I start to think a bit about old age and declining competence when I spot a small hand-printed note on the pump that says "Credit card broken—pay cash." I see a young lady in a pill box like structure up ahead and hope she can tell me what to do.

"Hi! Do I pay you?"

"Yep."

"Before or after?"

"Now."

I dig in my pocket and find only $17 – enough cash to get about the length of three football fields. Gerry's in the lady's room with our serious money. A line starts to form. I try to stall. "Tough job?"

She looks at me suspiciously like maybe I remind her of her former probation officer.

I continue the stall. "Lots of pissed-off people, eh?"

She flashes a nice smile. "You better believe it baby."

I pump 17 dollars' worth of $4.39/gal gas and start the RV up. WHAT! Yes! START UP! A block from home we pass our neighbors, the Vaccaros, who wave and cheer as if we are returning from Cranston, Rhode Island, or somewhere important like that. I turn the engine off in our driveway then turn the key back on. IT STARTS!

Epilogue

I bet you are just dying to find out why the RV kept stalling. It was a fuel pump that failed intermittently when it got hot. The pump is located in the gas tank which requires the gas tank to be drained to be fixed. My guess is that most mechanics would be reluctant to risk an expensive and risky diagnoses to a transient customer. All I can say is it's nice to be home! It is indeed nice to be back home. We look forward to June when the whole family will be together for a while. Mike, Bren, Diamond, and Lizzie are here now. Jack will soon be back from Ireland and James from Buenos Aires.

Mike Tyson was filming an episode of *Dancing with the Stars* in Buenos Aires and was on James's flight. I read an article last month on how Mike has completely changed his life. No more chewing on ears. The title of the article is "I've Learned to Live a Boring Life." Amen to that brother.

Jack's Limericks

There once was a poet named Sonny
Who hoped to write limericks for money
He spent most of the time
chasing a rhyme
Starvation! It really ain't funny
###
There once was a man who claimed Jesus was kin
Who just knew Trump was going to win
With God on his side
and PACs right behind
He said a vote for Joe Biden was a sin
###
There once was a party called GOP
that preached trickle-down misery
They just knew all those takers
Were nothing but fakers
Let's make GOP history

13

Jack's Shouts & Murmurs

LET IT GO! (What's the Worst That Can Happen?)

This piece is best shouted in the southern call and response style of born again Christians and other sinners who can shout real good!

Here goes:

That $100/month storage unit stuffed with moldy furniture from your children's failed marriages?
LET IT GO! OR GET OVER IT!

That advice you're going to give your teenage daughter who is now 42 and working on her fourth marriage?
LET IT GO!

That stack of "Shit Happens" and "Make America Great Again" bumper stickers?
LET IT GO!

That hour long video of your 2 year old taken by your four year old?

AND

All those boring sunset videos?

AND

That Super 8 movie of the birth of your eleven pound son?
LET IT GO!

That rhinestone roach clip wedding present?
LET IT GO!

The cell phone number of that cute guy you woke up with the morning after your retirement party?
LET IT GO!

All those useless computers, printers, cables, chargers, 1200 baud modems, cyan and magenta ink cartridges, unlabeled CDs, Windows 98 tutorials, Visicalc?
LET IT GO!

That baby raccoon your son found while hitchhiking back from Montana?
LET IT GO!

That loaded Glock you keep under your pillow to protect you from home invasions and pushy young Mormons?
LET IT GO!

That AK 47 you keep by the door to protect you and your loved ones from aliens and tyrannical governments?
LET IT GO!

That lawsuit against your divorce lawyer?

AND

That lawsuit against your pastor?
LET IT GO!

AND

That men's Stars & Stripes Speedo bathing suit?

AND

Those guaranteed combo weight loss and erectile dysfunction pills?

AND

That damn scale in the bathroom?
LET IT GO!

This list?
LET IT GO

That 1968 VW engine rusting out behind the garage?
LET IT GO!

That 80 year old boyfriend who calls you by his dead wife's nickname—Bunny?
LET IT GO!

Those red high heels you keep just in case you get invited back to another office party?
LET IT GO!

That boxed set of ancient Gaelic turnip recipes?
LET IT GO!

That Hip Hop for Dummies book?
LET IT GO!

You lost the last election and you lost the Civil War?
GET OVER IT!

A Geezer's Lament

- ✓ I remember when you dialed a phone you talked to real people.
- ✓ I remember when we knew WE were going to heaven and THEY were going to hell.
- ✓ I remember when we trusted priests, believed cops, and feared the Vice Principal.
- ✓ I remember when we were proud meat and potatoes guys and smoking was pretty Kool.
- ✓ I remember when newspapers were made of paper.
- ✓ I remember when heart attacks killed and crutches were the only knee replacements.
- ✓ I remember when cancer, abortions, and suicide were secrets.
- ✓ I remember when grieving did not require medication.
- ✓ I remember when the opiate of the masses was religion not Zoloft or The NFL.
- ✓ I remember when the Ed Sullivan show would only show Elvis from the waist up.
- ✓ I remember when Rock & Roll threatened civilization.
- ✓ I remember when boxing was bigger than football.
- ✓ I remember when gambling and pot were illegal.
- ✓ I remember when the GOP were in a lather about deficits, Russia, and losing China.
- ✓ I remember when most hunters didn't know assault weapons were for the overthrow of a tyrannical US government.
- ✓ I remember when truth mattered, our elections were envied, and our country was truly great.

✓ I remember when a map of the US came in more colors than red and blue.

✓ I remember when we did not know about Sunni, Shia, Kurds, or Alawites and we could not care less.

✓ I remember when Tarzan was the smartest guy in the jungle … and Jane the smartest girl.

✓ I remember when we thought John Wayne was a hero, or was that Charlton Heston?

✓ I remember when our Marshall Plan helped us win the Cold War.

✓ I remember when everyone except Communists and Martians loved us.

✓ I remember when we were 4% of the world population enjoying 50% of its resources.

✓ I remember when Congress actually worked every now and then.

✓ I remember when most of us didn't know President Roosevelt spent most of his life in a wheel chair.

✓ I remember when it was our moral duty to beat up fags.

✓ I remember when Ronald Reagan refused to respond to the AIDS epidemic.

✓ I remember when the letters LGBTQ were only used on eye tests.

✓ I remember when Blacks and women knew their place and Hispanics were invisible.

✓ I remember when except for the Native Americans (*whose land we invaded*), most of our US ancestors were immigrants.

✓ I remember when we just knew we would be better off than our parents.

So many things in my life have changed but now it looks like that was only practice.

14

In Illness & in Health

Young Jack, before the fall. 1956.

STAIR TREK

I didn't think I was old enough to fall down the stairs. I was wrong. I'm often wrong but nonetheless I'm determined to find out how I came to kiss my basement floor quicker than you can say "Splat." I want to do one of those post-mortems. Like they do when a bunch of healthy, intelligent, type A people go for a hike on a sunny winter's day and end up a month later with one husky guy stumbling out of the woods on severely frostbit feet mumbling how he only ate them after they were dead—his fellow hikers not his feet. The backup AA batteries our footless

Mr. Stumps forgot to bring for his GPS were the innocuous little detail that resulted in me break-dancing down the basement stairs. It was a life threatening event. All I wanted to do was turn off the TV after watching seven episodes of *Trailer Park Boys* on Netflix.

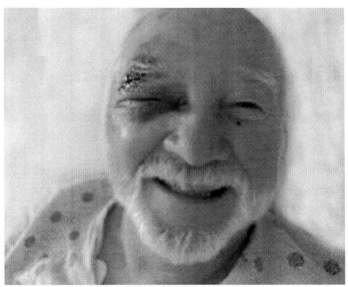

Jack - after the fall. Circa 2015.

We know most disasters are the consequences of an accumulation of large and small decisions that somehow come together to laugh at our plans and assumptions. In this case the primary determinant started over a year ago when I was in Wal-Mart. Yes, Wal-Mart. I saw a stack of step-in slippers on sale for $9.99. I had been looking for a pair of step-ins because I no longer am sure I can straighten up after bending over to tie or buckle more high class slippers. My shoe size is about 10/11 but the size 10/11 I tried on was too tight. The chance of being spotted in Wal-Mart was increasing with every minute, so I grabbed a size 12/13 without even trying them on. The sticker said "Made in China" so I figured size 12/13 Made-in-China slippers would fit my Made in USA feet just fine.

Back home I almost gloated as I stepped into them without having to bend over. But, for some reason, they irritated my feet. After a few days of pain I felt inside and found a stiff piece of cardboard stuffed into each slipper to make them look more desirable to slipper needy consumers like me. With the cardboard removed the spacious slippers became schleppers. For the next year I schlepped hundreds maybe thousands of times up and down those basement stairs usually overloaded with food and drink as we ate our way through the whole series of *The West Wing*. Every time I schlepped on those stairs, I told myself that I just had to sneak to Wal-Mart and get me a pair of size 10/11. Late on a warm September day, I suddenly stopped telling myself that. Instead I wondered why I was lying on the floor while a group of EMT folks were cutting my pants off. I don't remember much of that night but I do remember being unable to ask them where they got such great scissors.

One of the cruelties plaguing the human condition is that many of us are given one dimensional brains to make our way in a multi-dimensional world. That's why so many scientists use multivariate equations to figure things out. That's why so many self-help books fail dismally. The self-help author may have a good premise but is so taken up with the brilliance of his/her premise he/she ignores or attacks any other related good premises. Hence, while the Schlepper premise is certainly valid, we must rigorously examine other possible factors that resulted in my befriending gravity.

For example, another factor may have been the unintended consequences caused by my neighbor's thoughtfulness and generosity. In early September, he had four enormous yellow maple trees cut down and had the tree guys leave all the firewood for me. Here were several cords of wood within a hundred feet of my wood stove. I was in firewood locavore heaven. I wanted to show my generous neighbor how grateful I was by cutting and moving all the wood and cleaning up his yard ASAP. I even bought a new $400 Stihl chainsaw when my forty year old Stihl faltered. By the time it got dark I had a lot of wood cut to size. The day was warm, my clothes were soaked and my throat was parched. Another way to say I was dehydrated, deserved a hot shower, and a nice glass of wine or two.

These factors were at play the night I found myself in the South County Hospital Emergency room where I finally regained consciousness.

I can tell you from bitter experience, consciousness is a bummer! It made me aware of my wife Gerry and what she must be going through. She did not deserve this. I deserved this but knew damn well I would be alright even though I couldn't see out of one eye and my head was banging like a blacksmith on meth. Denial can be a friend.

This was the first time in my life that I got good news before I was aware of any bad, for example, after the second CAT scan at Rhode Island Hospital the neurosurgeon determined that my hematoma was not expanding, so I probably would not need brain surgery. My theory was that all the extra blood drained into the cavity that used to store my working memory. I also got the good news from the ophthalmologist that even though I cracked my eye socket in a few places, the cracks would not hinder the operation of my eye. I still would be able to see the runaway garbage truck hurtling at me from that side street. I could even still wink.

But, the good news came at a price. In order to confirm that my skull was harder than the basement floor the ophthalmologist felt she had to have a look-see in my eye—the eye that was swollen shut—shut tight. She tried a number of times to roll my eyelid up. My sister once worked for an eye surgeon and found that for several common procedures, most men require sedation while most women do not. That along with a pronounced aversion to pain, especially when I can only see out of one blurry eye, puts me well into the 90 percentile of CMES (Chicken Male Eyeball Syndrome).

Yet, this woman was persistent. After failing to get my eyeball naked with her fingers she pulls two chopsticks from her bag and after a few tries, rolls my top eyelid back with one chopstick. Then, holding the other chopstick with the same hand, rolls my lower eyelid down. She then reaches in her bag for what looks like a playing card. You know, like those cards with pictures of dogs smoking cigars and playing poker. Next she reaches in her bag and with the same hand that's holding the card, pulls out a small magnifying glass and places the card in front of my swollen terror stricken eye. Now I get it. It's an eye test.

Holding two eyelids open with one hand and holding an eye test while moving the magnifying glass with the other hand she shouts something. I hear, "LAN FA! LAN FA" but I think I understand because I'm hard of hearing and often have to fill in a lot of blanks. I try to find line 4.

No luck! I shout, "ARHHG, ARHHG CAN'T ARHHG SEE"

She tries again "LAN TREE! LAN TREE."

Desperate, I fake it "ABCDE!"

"NO! NO! NUMBUS! NUMBAS!"

Again, I say "ARHHG, ARHHG CAN'T ARHHG SEE."

She sighs "OKAY" and slowly repacks her instruments. I see the chopsticks are really cotton swab sticks.

Our tryst at an end, I fall back onto the bed—spent but strangely aroused. She looks into my good eye smiles a shy smile and whispers "See you tomorrow." I can hardly wait.

PALPITATIONS

In 1993 I had two heart attacks. The first time I woke up at 5 am with mild cramps in my biceps. Until then I considered myself and my biceps to be indestructible. Without thinking a whole lot about the details, I was sure I would live forever, sure that "they" were going to find a cure in my lifetime for whatever might come at me. I also considered myself a sort of Atheist Christian Scientist and was proud that I had not seen a doctor since my army days thirty years earlier.

I still think it's remarkable that on this fine June morning I sense something different, something important happening. So, despite ignoring doctors all these years for pneumonia, flu, Lyme, broken foot, bad knees, etc., I gently shake Gerry's shoulders and tell her I want to go to the hospital. Perhaps it's her relief that I don't have something else on my mind, but whatever, she responds as if I'm asking her to accompany me to Cumberland Farms to get a half gallon of milk and the morning paper.

The hospital's about twenty minutes away and with each passing minute I realize this event is indeed important. My biceps are now aching, and I have a powerful pain in my chest. We stop at a red light. I want to scream at Gerry to just go through the stupid fucking light! She makes a complete stop at every stop sign. Just blow through them for Christ sakes! There's no one on the road at this hour—this, the hour I'm going to die! But I don't want to get her worried. About half way there I begin to sweat and feel nauseous. I lean over and tell Gerry I love her and have no money hidden anywhere.

She responds "Uh Huh." like we're deciding whether we should get 1% or 2% milk at Cumby's.

Gerry drops me off at the Emergency Room entrance and goes to park the car. I lurch through the doors and tell the receptionist "I think I'm having a heart attack!" While they take a blood test, the pain everywhere is getting much worse. I'm having trouble breathing. I assume they're going to crack my chest. I'm pretty sure I'm going to die.

That's when the doctor comes in and announces "Mr. Barry, you are indeed having a myocardial infarction, a heart attack, and here is what we're going to do. This IV we're giving you contains a number of medications to relieve your pain and break the blockage that's causing your heart attack." And here's the really wonderful thing he says, *"Mr. Barry, IN TWENTY MINUTES YOU'LL BE GOOD AS NEW."* Did I hear correctly? I'm going to die! Right?

I never heard of TPA (Tissue Plasminogen Activator). It's amazing the stuff you learn about as you get older. In twenty minutes I am indeed as good as new. I understand the IV included a dab of morphine but that's not what makes this one of the best days of my life. I spend the next few days in the ICU watching Michael Jordan shred the Suns in the NBA playoffs. I'm beginning to see things a little differently now. I wonder when Mr. Jordan's going to learn about TPA.

Six months later I'm raking leaves when I get those feelings again. This time I end up in Rhode Island Hospital for an angioplasty. Gerry asks Dr. McKindal, a handsome young man right out of central casting, if he has done many of these things before. He says not to worry he's going watch the training video at home tonight. The blockage is in a tough place. When they blow up the balloon to squish the blockage open it feels like a heart attack. For this spot they need to squish a lot. I tell them "Fire away lads!" I wish I had thought of the sniff/puff Lamaze exercise to get me past all the squishing. As an award for staying alive, they give me a popsicle. No popsicle ever tasted so good.

Seventeen years later, putting my shirt back on after my annual cardiac checkup, I mention that I get some funny feelings only when I start to bike or XC ski. After I get warmed up I'm okay. Dr. Ferra, my cardiologist, says "Now you tell me." Sure enough a stress test shows I need to clean the pipes again. Hello Dr. McKindal. He looks to have aged a lot better than me.

Friends in my URI spinning class bought me a heart monitor so I'll know what my heart is up to. It's a Timex. I remember an early TV news anchor intoning "It takes a licking and keeps on ticking" in old Timex ads. This digital Timex comes in two parts. One part goes around your chest sort of like a training bra for elderly men. It sends your heart rate to a wristwatch that can tell time. When you set it to heart monitor mode, it tells you how fast your heart is beating. All this sounds simple enough but one day this device almost gave me a heart attack. It was in the 1:00 spinning class. Spinning consists of stationary bikes, bad music, and athletic spin Nazis. Well, at least my playlist is superior.

With the help of beta blocker pills I seldom go above 120 heart beats a minute. Everything is fine until with about twenty minutes to go I notice my heart rate is up to **125**. I start to keep an eye on it. It slowly climbs to **130**. I surreptitiously ease up on the pedal tension. It's not like I'm competitive or anything, but I'll be damned if I let any of those slackers around me think I'm cheating. **135!** Damn! I slow down, but not so much that anyone would notice. A few minutes later **138!** Other than being scared to death I feel ok. What the hell is going on? **139!** It just keeps going up, slow but steady. **140!** Thank God! Time for cool down! Let's just coast. Wait a minute! **142!** How can that be, I'm only coasting? I begin to worry that if I die, I'll fall off the goddam bike. What a bloody mess! Will I bleed if my heart stops beating before I hit the floor? Time to dismount and stretch. I ease off the bike; feet touch the floor; I still feel ok; but my little Timex says otherwise. **144!** Should I ask for help? Stretching is over. We all clap. Is clapping the last thing I'll ever do? I'm thinking I'll ask my buddy Scott to tell my wife and kids that I love them and I'm sorry. Sorry for what, does not cross my mind. I turn and look up at the wall clock behind me. **1:45 pm**.

OTHER LIES

15

GUNS & MORE GUNS

FORTY-FIVE

Homer Mason's brother Cicero robbed a bank. It didn't take long for him to get caught, but the cops never did find the gun he used. That's because Homer had it, which meant, the kids in the neighborhood had it. The cops didn't find it because it floated from kid to kid in a system more like trading comics than like any real plan to hide it. You get to share the gun if you're one of the boys. But Cicero's gun taught me that guns are trouble.

We're in the meadows down by the Connecticut River. It's mostly scrub growth, mud and abandoned cars and refrigerators. Mike Duggan has the gun—a forty-five pistol. It's big. Interstate 91 has just been built. It doesn't take homeless people long to set up shop under the new bridges. We don't call them homeless, so we don't think of them as homeless. We call them bums and think of them as bums. They're the enemy. This is not unusual. In our world just about every adult, every kid outside the project, and every older kid from the project is the enemy. On this particular day we're at war with the bums. When we get to the bridge it looks like no one's around. Muddy mattresses, mounds of wet blankets, and a variety of cardboard boxes litter the camp. Rows of dead soldiers line the concrete bridge support ledges. We come upon a fire pit with a dead burnt cat in it. It doesn't occur to us that the cat may have been already dead when it was thrown in the fire. This sacrificial cat proves we're the good guys and the bums are flat-out evil. No one's joking now. An empty Thunderbird gallon wine bottle shines amongst other dead soldiers on the concrete ledge. As if shattering the bottle will shatter the evil, shatter our fear, Mike pulls the gun, aims, squeezes. The 45 sounds like a damn cannon under that bridge. The bullet pinging on steel adds a nervous high note to the bedlam. The bottle still sits there, deaf to it all, but a nearby pile of cardboard erupts. Two arms waving surrender poke through, then a head pops up, eyes blinking. Cardboard man is having trouble seeing in the bright sun. Slowly he lowers his arms, fussily wipes his coat and takes a wobbly step toward us. Mike wipes blood from his cheek where the pistol kicked back. "Hey kid! Gimme that gun." We all take a step back. "I'm undercover FBI. C'mere. I'll show you my badge." Another step back. "Gimme the gun kid or I'll sic J. Edgar Hoover on your sorry little ass." Mike laughs "Yo mama's undercover!" The bum starts to shuffle toward Mike. Mike raises the pistol. Mike's younger brother Johnny starts to cry. The bum stops short. "Then get the hell outta here you nasty little crybabies."

We run through the woods looking back to make sure the bum's not coming. After we catch our breath, Johnny starts to imitate the bum. "Hey kids! Me want gun! Me FBI big shit." Our laughter declares us victors wiping the slate clean of any crybaby fear or panic. Later I ask Mike, "What were you going to do if the bum kept coming?" Mike answers with a thin smile. "Blow his fucking head off man." Neither of us believe it. Later that afternoon, a dumb sparrow lands on a tree limb just above Mike. This time he holds the gun in both hands. Again the gun sounds like a cannon. Feathers fall lazily to the ground.

SEVENTEEN

Serena ran home from school as she did for the past two weeks. She ran up the front steps of the three-decker, opened the mailbox, and pumped her fist into the air. It's there! It's a fat envelope too! A good sign. Serena hesitated. *Should I open it here or wait to show Nana? What if it's bad news? Nah! It's got to be good.* She ran up to the second floor and pounded on the door. *Jeez. Why does Nana always keep the door locked? Anyone could kick it in if they wanted to.* Nana, busy at the sink, jumped when Serena pounded on the door, then peeked out the glass peek-hole.

Nana unlatched the three locks

"Seri! Don't you scare me like that."

"Sorry Nana but I got the letter."

"What does it say?"

"I don't know. I ain't opened it yet."

"Well c'mon Seri!"

Serena calmed herself. *Whatever this letter says, I'll still be here tomorrow. Still taking care of little brother Jojo, sister Maria, and even Nana.* Nana spoke little English and was afraid, afraid of cops, afraid of the case worker, afraid of men.

For Serena, the future held in that fat envelope began to sink in. *If I do go to Brown, it will just add to all the stuff I already do. But if you want to be a doctor ya gotta do what ya gotta do!* When Serena opened the envelope, she began to cry. Nana joined in with a wail.

Maria came out of the bedroom. "Hey! What's going on?"

"I got accepted to the Brown Head Start Program!"

Nana's wail got louder. Even though Nana couldn't read or write Serena handed her a thick packet of scholarship and financial aid forms. Nana smiled and pressed them to her breast. Jojo walked in the open door. "Mr. Lopez says he has his grill ready."

"Ready? What do you mean?" Serina asked.

"Your 17th birthday dummy! Mr. Lopez says he gets off work at five. He'll have everything ready by six. So be on time!"

A few blocks away Carlos sat in a car with Jose. They were from the Manton Project. Carlos was sixteen. Jose, twenty, was an enforcer in the Manton Bad Boyz gang. Carlos lay the pistol in his lap, surprised at how heavy it felt. "A Glock. A man's gun. Damn, I ain't ever even shot one off!"

Jose turned in the passenger seat of Carlos' car and smiled at him like a big brother.

"You the man now Carlos. You a Manton man. Got the ride. Got the piece. Got the tools. Know what I mean? You ready for business Carlos?"

"Believe it Jose."

"Yeah, I believe you Carlos. You just have to let this downtown badass Manuel know who we are. Send him a calling card. Know what

I mean?" Jose's smile was no longer a smile. "Stick with the plan. Know what I mean?" Jose gave Carlos a tight squeeze and left in his legal car.

Carlos was scared. He didn't want to be here but he knew he had few options—all of them bad. His mother had four kids. At seventeen, he was the man in the family. They couldn't afford to leave Manton Ave. He had to play by Manton rules. Serina came downstairs to join a small group of early arrivals. She noticed Mr. Lopez had brought his son Julio along. He was strong and handsome and knew it. He first saw Serena or rather first noticed her at her quinceañera when she was fifteen. Hey Serina. You're looking real fine today. Serina had mixed feelings regarding Julio and kept him at arms' length. "Oh, Hi Julio"

Carlos drove to the back of the three decker house, poked the Glock through the open window of the stolen car, braced his arm, took aim, shut his eyes, made a sign of the cross and squeezed the trigger. Serena bent over to get some Mexican street corn started. She never heard the shot that killed her.

ODYSSEY

<u>The Sale</u>

Honda Odyssey. 2000.

Jane read the church billboard again. "FREEDOM IS THE OXYGEN OF THE SOUL." Somehow it made her want another smoke. She tapped a Newport menthol from the pack and felt for her lighter. *I'll give her this last smoke then I'm out of here.* Jane didn't look like a woman who spent much time in church. As she approached her early forties, her smoking didn't help any. She had an athlete's body and moved like one. As if on cue, a white Honda Odyssey pulled into the parking lot. Jane stuffed the unlit cigarette into her coat pocket and smiled a thin smile. *Jesus! Afraid of getting caught smoking in a church parking lot. I must really be going off the deep end!*

The Honda Odyssey pulled up alongside Jane's beater. A plump, fortyish, sweat-is-the-enemy woman with perfect hair, Botoxed face, and white Burberry coat rolled down the window. Dolce & Gabbana Light Blue floated from the open window. "You must be Jane."

Jane didn't know the perfume but knew money when she smelled it. "Yeah, I'm Jane. I hope you're Gladys."

A nervous little chuckle then a loud "Lordy, Jane! I hope I am too."

Jane was relieved. *I don't know much about cars but I do know this lady has been well taken care of. The car is about as spotless as her coat.* Jane already decided to buy the car but thought it best to go through the negotiating routine. At $8,500 this was a steal and better yet, it would do the job.

"So Gladys, Why are you selling the car?"

"Well Jane, my husband George, has been transferred overseas. Paris no less."

Jane tried to sound enthusiastic "Wow Gladys! You must be so excited!"

Subdued, Gladys looked down then she looked past Jane. "You know Jane, I'm not so sure."

"Not so sure Gladys?"

Gladys frowned "Oh, I know they have good food and nice art over there but I've been told that men relieve themselves in broad daylight. Beggars actually touch you and then there's that funny language—like they all have sinus infections or something. You know I'm just not so sure."

"Any problems with the car that you know of Gladys?"

"We always brought the car in promptly for all its inspections and so forth. Brand new tires too. All the receipts are in the glove compartment. I numbered each one by date. Would you like to see them?"

"No Gladys, I believe you."

"Oh wait! There was one thing they somehow couldn't find a way to fix no matter how many times I told them. I do want to make sure I've been totally honest with you."

"What was the problem, Gladys?"

"Well the driver's seat belt occasionally gets in the way when you try to close the door. What a racket it makes sometimes. I brought it to three different dealers but they all said it's just the way it was designed and there wasn't anything they could do. Just make sure the seat belt's inside the car when you close the door they said. I actually thought of writing to Mr. Honda or whoever."

Jesus! Jane thought, *If only I had problems like that. Let's get on with this.* "Hey Gladys, I like your car. I am prepared to offer you $6,500 cash."

Gladys answered with a wavering but quick OKAY and looked relieved. "You know, Jane, this is the first time I did anything like this. I was so nervous. Craig's List and all that. George made me do it. Said negotiating would be good training for France. I don't know. You never know who you're going to be dealing with. Is there a Craig's List in France? I'm glad you're the one buying my car. You really seem to know what you're doing."

"I like you too, Gladys. Oh! One more thing before we take care of business." Jane took a tape measure from her purse and measured the distance from behind the driver's seat to the rear hatch. *It's a bit short but I can always put his body in on a diagonal or maybe saw his legs off if needed.* "OKAY Gladys let's get this show on the road."

The Plan

As soon as Jane got back to her apartment, she called her business partner Danny. Jane wanted to keep their relationship purely business because Danny was a control freak wannabe who was too frisky with his hands on women. Jane was recovering from a very bad marriage and felt she only needed money not sex at this phase of her life.

"Danny. I got us a car for the job."

"Jane, What did I tell ya? What did I goddam tell ya? Huh?"

"You told me not to use the phone Danny. Sorry, I forgot."

"See you in half an hour at the office, Jane."

The office was a bar called Panacea Bar & Grill where you could spend a lot of time just reading tattoos. Danny liked this intrigue stuff. Liked it almost as much as he liked killing people. Jane knew that she could never kill anyone but was surprised at how much the game excited her. And, the pay wasn't bad. Not bad at all. *And this job will be the biggest payday yet.*

Danny was in touch with the client, a lady with deep pockets—very deep pockets. The client wanted her husband George out of the way in the worst way and was clearly willing to pay. She knew her husband visited numerous kinky internet sites. She knew what he liked. Jane would be the bait—complete with red stiletto heels, lots of leather, and porno hardware—a call girl with a wide range of desires and imagination who would put George in heaven. The plan is to get him tied up in a bit of bondage foreplay. Danny shows up as the irate husband; shoots George; plants some meth on George; loads the body in the Odyssey. He meets the client at the river to inspect the job and pay for services rendered. Then Danny and Jane dump the body. Simple!

Well not exactly! Everything's going smoothly. Jane and George are enjoying their second glass of wine in a rent by the hour motel. Danny busts into the room before anyone's tied up. He raises the gun to shoot George. The long silencer on the 45 barrel hits the nightstand. The bullet goes through the fleshy part of George's thigh. For a pudgy little guy, George is quick and strong. He grabs the pistol out of Danny's hand by the long silencer and turns it on Danny. Jane hears Danny's finger break as his fake emerald ring gets stuck in the trigger guard. He starts to whimper. Jane thinks she sees George smile. Another shot. Danny teeters, looking surprised that he has a hole in his forehead. He falls across George knocking him to the floor. Without thinking she grabs her red shoe in a panic and swings with all her might. Slowly sinking to the carpet, blood gushing from behind his ear, George looks almost as surprised as Danny.

Jane sits on the bed, numb, her mind racing. Without Danny to help, she needs a plan B. She doesn't know how she ever got those bodies into the Odyssey. *Must be adrenaline.* By the time she gets to the river she's shaking, exhausted. She pulls up next to a large Mercedes. The window rolls down. Jane catches a familiar scent of expensive perfume. The client leans out the window.

I can't believe it "Gladys! What the hell are you doing here?"

"Lordy Jane, I was about to ask you the same thing."

"Gladys, I need your help."

"Well Jane, let's get this show on the road."

Both Jane and Gladys are panting and soaked in sweat when their work is done. Gladys is exhilarated. Even the sweat feels good. She turns to Jane and lifts her arm for a high five. Jane flinches—a reflex picked up from bully Danny—then Jane quickly recovers and hugs Gladys. Gladys leans closer. Jane feels Gladys's breath on her neck, and fills her hands with Gladys's hair then gently pulls Gladys to her. Everything goes quiet.

Jane quickly pulls back. "Jesus Gladys, I'm sorry! So embarrassed! I don't know what came over me. I'm not that kind ya know."

Gladys steps back and smiles wide. "Lordy Jane! Me either! But I do think I finally got my money's worth out of that expensive Dolce perfume. I might just buy another bottle. Wanna dance?"

Jane laughs.

"Jane, come on home with me."

"Let's get this show on the road, Gladys."

Panacea Liquidators, LLC

Months later Gladys is lying in bed giving Jane a sleepy little massage. "Wow Jane! Not an ounce of fat on you. Where'd you get all these muscles in your back?"

Jane slowly turns her head sideways and mumbles lazily into the pillow "Jeeze Gladys, how would I know? I've had over seventy different jobs in my life."

"No!"

"Yep! I counted them once. Took me forever to remember and list them all. Even now something will pop into my head and I'll add another job to the list. So maybe it was driving that cement truck or maybe the pole dancing I did."

"Maybe pole dancing, Jane?"

Jane rolls over. "My back Gladys! All those muscles you seem to like so much—I could of got them pole dancing."

"Pole dancing?"

"Yeah! Let me tell you Jane, pole dancing can be goddam hard on your back. I lasted about three months. Cold cocked a real persistent guy. I forgot I had a Corona beer bottle in my hand at the time."

Gladys says softly "Pole dancing? Cement trucks? Whoa Jane."

Jane rolls back onto her stomach. "A little lower, Gladys. Oh yeah! Right there."

George's estate provided Gladys and Jane with, as they say, a comfortable life. Gladys had a bit of trouble with George's insurance because there was no body. There was proof he spent a lot of time in leather bars. But further investigation turned up dry. Then one summer day an old lady fishing for catfish along the Connecticut River down by Fish Fry Street found an enormous dead snapping turtle. The turtle was a legend among local fishermen and kids. They called him "Sir Toes" because of his age and eating habits. Sir Toes evidently died trying to swallow a finger. The finger didn't kill him, but swallowing that huge fake emerald ring did. Although the insurance company maintained that the finger did not prove that George was one hundred percent dead, the ring along with DNA tests did yield another million to the final settlement.

Gladys felt responsible for Toes, and was out of sorts for days. She donated $10,000 to Save the Connecticut River and another $5,000 to the Ecuadorian Estuarine Turtle Institute. She began to think about using turtles to make their services more environmentally friendly. She wanted to review best practices for body disposal and recycling. Gladys even took a trip to Varanasi, India where bodies are cremated on the Ganges River and massive turtles finish off the remains of loved ones. For the first time in a long time, each woman, in her own way, started to look ahead. And that's how Panacea Liquidators LLC was formed.

Jane and Gladys became regulars at The Panacea Bar & Grill as they patrolled Curves, Zumba, Tia Chi, martial arts, Pilates, even yoga classes, all those wellness places packed with women busting their asses to keep hubby from straying, or to attract a man who might fill the void left by a straying hubby. Gladys even picked up a good customer in The Happy Nose Aroma Therapy Emporium. It didn't hurt that the customer's name was Daisy or that her partner would snort anything Daisy blew her way. That's when Jane and Gladys learned about the dangerous Caster Bean plant and its poison product ricin.

As for marketing, all they had to do was complain over diet lattes about how bad their make believe husbands treated them and sit back and listen to stories about real husbands. Stories that would make your skin crawl. On average it would take about three weeks of lattes before the talk turned serious. Business boomed.

16

THEM & US

GAZA

I handed her the photo. She held it inches from her good eye. She took a quick step back. "Yes! That's me in the photo." Without me asking, she told me her story. Sometimes in quick bursts, sometimes slowly. Always with pain. "We were living in the city of Beit Lahiya in Gaza back those many years ago. We grew strawberries in the l-Atatra neighborhood. We were happy then. But, not after that day. I remember August 14, 2014 as if it was today. How could I not? I see it, feel it, smell it, hear it still. It was Friday, the day of prayer. Bombs were dropping everywhere. The sky was also thick with missiles flying toward Israel. Eleven-thousand homes in Gaza were destroyed. Seventy percent of the people in Gaza were now refuges. My father brought us to an abandoned school. There would be no bombs there. Then he left to join a small band of men carrying shovels and rifles. He held us to him for a moment but did not say where he was going. I never saw him again. I never heard the blast that leveled the school. I awoke outside the hospital to my sister Farah's screaming. Farah was a simple but happy girl. My father said she was a gift from God. Her name means joy and she brought us much joy. But that day she had burns over most of her back. Her hair was gone. She did not understand the pain. She did not understand why no one helped her. We did not understand triage. The shame I felt was that I did not help her and I felt relief when she stopped screaming."

My heart leapt when I saw my mother Gharam. Her name means "Love." Father always joked she loved us too much. She should save some for Allah. She walked right past us as if we did not exist. I ran to her. I called her name. She continued walking. A small trickle of blood ran from each ear. I tugged at her cloak. She looked down at me then continued walking. Gharam lived for three more years but never uttered another word. For me, this was the day my loving mother died.

They had put a patch over my left eye. It did nothing to relieve the pain, a pain so great I could think of nothing else. I do remember a fair-skinned man taking photographs. I remember he had real shoes not sandals. They were tan, covered with blood. Funny what you see as a child. What you remember. I have never seen this photograph before. Yes! It is me but, I don't want it. I don't know that little girl. She's gone! She died fifty years ago, and here we are in 2064 still killing each other.

VICTIMS

In my relatively short time on this earth I have observed that many people who do bad things see themselves as victims, often self-righteous victims. This happens in families. It happens between countries. It happens between cultures. I am surprised that with all the attention paid to bullying, I don't hear much about this universal thread of victimhood. For example citizens of post-World War I Germany were victims of the Treaty of Versailles, a harsh and punitive treaty fueled by the horrors of trench warfare that stripped Germany of 25,000 square miles of territory and seven million citizens. It called for reparations that bankrupted the defeated country. Those scratchy old films showing Germans carting useless money in wheelbarrows may seem quaint today but the desolation and humiliation Germans experienced after WWI helped sow the evil seeds for WWII.

The Holocaust created many millions of victims. Not only those who died but also those who survived. Even the generation following the Holocaust was scarred. Israel now finds itself immersed in an existential battle surrounded by enemies. It certainly needs to defend itself from the onslaught of missiles fired on its people. But anyone looking at recent images of a flattened Gaza, sees victims. Collateral damage is the enemy of civilization. Some of these victims are sure to create more victims. Israel finds itself in the difficult role of Goliath while David fires his slingshot from Gaza.

These observations are not intended to weigh in on the many controversies surrounding the Israeli/Palestinian dispute. These disputes do appear small given what's at stake for entire peoples, and entire cultures. Unfortunately the examples of victimization above are but a small sample of a depressingly endless catalog of our alacrity and exuberance for creating victims. I do not purport that all wars are bad or that I can tell you which ones are good. The few examples presented here are used to make the point that we Homo Sapiens seem to have a limited ability to see past our narrow self-interests but a boundless capability to rationalize our behavior. I certainly do not want to create another bully. But I also don't want to become a bully because I see myself as victim. I try to remember that every time I want to smack some bully upside the head. If you see yourself as victim, beware!

As W. H. Auden cautioned:

> *I and the public know*
> *What all schoolchildren learn,*
> *Those to whom evil is done*
> *Do evil in return.*

SILENCE

We kids knew the USA was the best country in the world. We were free. Anyone could be president. We were the good guys. Bing Crosby, Bob Hope, Johnny Weissmuller, and John Wayne informed my world view. I'm no longer a kid and have come to the realization that things are a bit more complicated. For example: How does my country deal with genocide? We certainly have had plenty of opportunity to showcase our values, values that make us exceptional, values that explain why God likes us best. But, in the face of the extermination of whole peoples and their culture, we often respond with self-interest, with silence. A silence broken only by empty words and clucking tongues.

Let's start with the one million Armenians in 1915. Silence! We didn't want to get involved in WWI.

Then there are the six million Jews in Europe. Silence! We didn't want to get distracted from our truly noble response to state sponsored fascist aggression in WWII. Evidently, this fear of distraction often kept us from providing Jewish people refuge in this country during WWII.

In the late seventies the Khmer Rouge, led by Pol Pot, killed more than two million Cambodians. For years our government and much of our mainstream media refused to believe the horrific reports of mass murder killing fields coming from escaped refugees. After the 1979 Vietnam invasion of Cambodia provided irrefutable proof of the atrocities, we continued to support the inclusion of Pol Pot's emissaries to the United Nations for another three years, three years Pol Pot spent in hiding. Silence! We were still mad at Vietnam for winning the Vietnam War. Evidently we didn't want to upset our newly found friends in China who backed Pol Pot while the Soviet Union backed the Vietnamese in Cambodia.

Up to 5,000 Kurds were gassed to death in 1988 as part of Iraq's Al-Anful campaign. It was the largest chemical weapons attack directed against civilians in history. Silence, while we quietly doubled our funding to Saddam Hussein. We were mad at the Ayatollah in Iran for taking over our embassy.

In Rwanda, Hutu exterminated 800,000 Tutsi in 1994. Tutsis responded in kind. Silence! Bureaucratic infighting and fear of a repeat of Somalia where the bodies of several US military were dragged through the streets of Mogadishu inhibited any response. In retrospect President Clinton has stated that the "biggest regret" of his presidency was not acting decisively to stop the Rwandan genocide.

Speaking of President Clinton, our response to mass killings in the Balkans in the 1990s was delayed for a year or more of carnage. Republicans along with the righteous Democratic Senator Joe Lieberman were too busy protecting us from oral sex in the executive branch.

There are all too many more examples, but, some of those are in Africa so what the hell. After all, now we know they're just shithole countries. Recent additions to this horrific list include:

- Bashar al-Assad and Syria and Vladimir Putin bombing Syrian rebels and civilians;
- Rohingya Genocide in Myanmar;
- Donald Trump's abandoning our Kurd allies to Turkey;
- Mohammed bin Salman's proxy war in Yemen.

All too often, more people die from the squalor, lawlessness, and disease born of displacement than die from the initial mayhem. Of course this may be confused with 20/20 hindsight, so why bring it up.

Silence has been our policy from the beginning, creating fog as thick as Henry Kissinger's accent. All I am saying is we might make better decisions if we understand that the world is complicated, that we almost always act in our own self-interest, and all too often we are not much different than the other guy.

THE WATCHER

This story was written several years ago before drones replaced boots-on-the-ground as a foreign policy tool.

There he goes again. Still carrying that package or is it a different one this time. For some reason the kid reminded Travis of himself when he was ten. A kid full of energy, always smiling—street dust, swirling around him. Travis was watching him, watching everyone else in the square too. It was his job, third shift, mostly boring, tedious.

At first glance this town square seemed completely different than West Virginia where Travis grew up. But then, the more he watched, maybe it wasn't so different. Mothers herding kids, young men strutting for the girls, bright-eyed girls making a show of not noticing, grownups noticing grownup things. Not much different than the Highland Mall back in Wheeling. But Travis was long gone from West Virginia. Long gone from his beating, beaten-down abusing father, his fearful mother, his younger sister who was about to be married, about to repeat the family dance of fear and anger. Travis was proud that he was the first in his family to break the chain of compromise and defeat, the first to graduate from college. Not just any college either—the Air Force Academy.

Whoa let me tell ya! This fucking kid is definitely sneaking packages into that house across the square. Each package about the size of a loaf of bread. INTEL had picked up an increase in foot traffic around the house. The kid wasn't smiling now. Neither was Travis. The kid's body language was tense, furtive. Travis focused on the house but couldn't see inside the shuttered windows. On the kids' next trip Travis saw that he was getting the packages from a beat up white van. The license plate was from a southern province. Adrenaline began to flow. *These goddamn people would use kids, goats, dogs anything!* Travis entered the password and code. Heads raised throughout the room. Colonel Burke peered over his shoulder. "What's up lieutenant?" Travis reran the last half hour. "Bastards! Using kids again. I'll put you on yellow. Just give a holler and you got the green light. And, make sure you document the whole goddam engagement lieutenant!"

Travis always wanted to be a fighter pilot. But competition was fierce. He worked hard in flight school. Even made it to the final cut. When he was accepted at the Air Force Academy he never imagined he'd end up doing this. Hell! He never even knew this stuff existed. This could be his first green light, an alert that would go all the way to the Pentagon. Travis was scared. *My first solo flight was nowhere as bad as this. It was tough as hell, but I was certain that if I did things right, followed protocol things would be alright. But what's the right thing right now? What the fuck is certain?*

The kid appeared again this time with four men carrying heavy boxes. Travis requested the green light. *If these jokers go out the back door I'll have to act fast.* He thought about the kid. He thought about the hundreds of people in the square. He zoomed in and locked the front door of the house on target. He thought he heard shots. He broke a sweat. A finger on the proverbial trigger so to speak. The next minute seemed an hour. That's when he saw the bride. Dressed in traditional silk, in a procession followed by dancing whirling clansmen beating drums and throwing firecrackers, the kid dancing in the middle of all the mayhem, his smile back. *The bride riding a camel no less, it was bread after all! Just goddam bread! No IED, nobody blown all to hell!*

Travis banked the drone left sending it high into the cloudless sky, back to home base. With no place to go, adrenaline made Travis lightheaded, bordering on nausea. His leg jiggled nervously. Good thing his shift was almost over. Stepping outside the Command Center into the parking lot, the desert sun made his eyes water. Good thing that even at 7am you could always get a good stiff cold one in Las Vegas.

Loose Ends

Sock Man

This story is told in the form of an ancient Japanese folk tale where a samurai is killed, his treasure stolen, and wife raped by bandits. The story is told from several very different perspectives. The tale was made into a film Rashomon *directed by Akira Kurosawa in 1950. Paul Newman made a spaghetti western* The Outrage *using the* Rashomon *plot. My version is sort of a ghetto* Rashomon. *The events as told by the narrator are true as far as I can recall. A warning! This story reflects the limited social perspective of a twelve-year-old wise guy in the 1950s. Have fun!*

The Narrator's Version

It never occurred to the cops that Johnny was a fulltime B&E man. He was at least six foot four and weighed a sloppy two hundred pounds. He always had a big cross hanging around his neck. So, maybe he'd make a good bouncer, but definitely not someone who could climb up roofs and squeeze through windows without waking everyone up. Maybe that's why it took so long to nail him.

He might still be at it, but he had this thing about socks. Stole every sock in sight. Didn't matter if they fit him or not. Hell, he even stole girl's socks. Project girls would line up after one of his shopping sprees downtown. What did him in was he would exchange socks when he broke into a house. That's right! Didn't matter if folks were at home as long as he could still hear them snoring, snug in their beds. He did this many times. Yeah, check it out! It was in the *Hartford Courant* back then. Nabbing socks along with the loot was his M.O., his signature. Sock Man! But this time, he's in someone's bedroom with his shoes off when someone starts screaming. All hell breaks loose. Johnny jumps over a laundry basket, hits his head on the door frame and knocks himself out cold.

Eddy's Version

It's the middle of the night. I'm having trouble falling to sleep. Must be hungover. I think I hear a noise. Hey man! It is a noise, like a drawer opening. I look up and see this giant. It looks like he's getting dressed or something. He's a giant alright but I got my piece, the great equalizer. I'll blow his goddam head off. Then I remember. I'm shacking up with Ruby May and she won't tolerate no guns at her house. So, I guess it's me and the giant. I reach up and tap him on the shoulder. "Hey man! What the fuck you doing here? You better get out before I get mad!" This guy is big but he's soft. I could smell the fear. "Know what I mean?" Big guy whispers something like "Okay, Okay" and runs toward the door. I give him a good swift kick in the ass, he stumbles into the door frame. Out cold! I tie him up and call the cops. I tell Angela the hot dispatch chick all the gory details. Then I tie up Big Guy real good. I can't wait for Walker, the world's dumbest probation officer, to see me in action. Maybe he'll stop giving me so much shit. Ha! I love it!

Ruby May's Version

It was Eddy that woke me up. We had been out late and I was still a little woozy from the booze and weed. Maybe this was punishment. Maybe the nuns were right. Maybe I should get married—even to Eddy. Make it legal and all. But, to tell the truth, I don't trust the little S.O.B. Hell! Maybe I don't even like him.

And, now I hear Eddy whining. "Hey! Big fella, Don't hurt me! I won't call no cops!" Skinny little no-ass Eddy must of scarfed down at least ten of those enchiladas last night. I just don't know where he puts it all. Hey, it don't make me no never mind, he deserves his nightmares. But, all of a sudden this giant monster stands up. Holy shit cakes! He must be seven feet tall. Takes up the whole damn room! Like Sassquish or whatever! I just catch a flash. He's jumping through the doorway when BAM! This giant asshole runs right into the door. His feet go up. His head snaps back. He's horizontal heading for the floor. Another BAM! but this time, a lot louder.

Now Eddy's yelling at me. Something about his guns. I yell back "Hey Eddy! Shut the fuck up and call the cops! I'll hide the weed." I just want to get out of this room but I'm afraid to step on Sassquish laying there. Jesus! He's snoring! As big as he is, he's kinda cute. Looks peaceful, like a baby that just got his diaper changed. Oh my god! He got no shoes on! And those stupid socks with the green shamrocks! Looks just like Eddy's Saint Patrick's speedo outfit. What was in that weed anyhow? I think I'm gonna tell Eddy to move out.

Officer O'Connor's Version

At 2:13AM, I receive an emergency alert on the squawk box identifying Apartment D, 211 Benevolent Avenue for what sounds like a home invasion. Hot Angela the dispatcher wasn't too sure. She says "Watch yourself, Connor. The caller was kinda squirrelly. We don't want anyone hurt do we?" Hey! Is Angela hitting on to me or what?

When I get to the address, I find an incoherent white male and a white female downstairs. No indication of any domestic altercation. The female is not at all hard to look at. Upstairs I find a very large light skinned Black man semiconscious on the floor tied up with several hundred feet of clothesline rope along with what appears to be an entire roll of duct tape on his legs. I apply handcuffs. It takes a while to remove the useless rope and tape. That's ok because it doesn't take me long to figure out this is the Sock Man. My lucky day! I can see it now. "Officer Brendan O'Connor apprehends the notorious Sock Man—twice his size!" I need some time to get a little more creative on the report. There may be a promotion in this. For the life of me I can't imagine how that little squirrel downstairs knocked this guy out.

Johnny The Sock Man's Version

"Where am I? What happened? Man, does my head hurt! Can't move my arms. These handcuffs hurt. Handcuffs! Handcuffs?... Damn! I'm caught. Caught after all this time. Maybe it's for the best. Just not worth it anymore. And, that Louie is a crook. Pays me a dime on the dollar for all the stuff he fences for me. I'm busting my ass just so he can send his kids to those I. V. colleges. I got kicked out of my school in the eighth grade. Yeah… Stealing gym socks. I wonder, do they have schools in jail?

Anyway, by now I'm mainly doing it for the socks. Don't really know why. Give most of them away to folks in the project. They said I was the Robin Hood of socks. Big Lucy even made a little doo wop number. Called it "Smiling Toes, Happy Feet."

Now I see this nice couple looking all scared. I never got to really meet who I robbed before. I never thought about them really. Now my head hurts even more. Maybe I should give them their socks back. They're kinda ugly anyway… The socks I mean.

But Mama! Oh man! Mama! She's going to be so hurting. She loves me so much and look what I done gone and did. It was hard enough that she married a Black man and worse yet, she drove a garbage truck. She's strong alright but I don't know. And Daddy, he works so hard. Took an extra job just to feed me when I was growing so fast. I wonder how much food you get in jail? Maybe if I confess to everything and give up Louie, they won't tell Mama and Daddy.

Man, I'm feeling so bad!

THE DUNNING LETTER

The summer I was ten Ronny St. Laurent's mother and her boyfriend occasionally took us to Barkhamsted Reservoir in western Connecticut. One time Ronny and I found a wallet in the parking lot of the lake concession stand. It was a beat up but shiny leather wallet, looking like it spent most of its life in the back pocket of a tight pair of Levis. I forget how much money there was in the wallet, but I do remember it was enough for each of us to scarf down a foot long hot dog with the works including the classy addition of crispy bacon. It was the best hot dog I ever had.

The main reason I can't remember the exact amount of money in the wallet was the priceless treasure we found in its folds. This included a Trojan, a picture of a woman naked from the waist up, and a single-spaced typed letter folded many times in order to fit in the wallet. The letter was a spoof reply to a dunning letter. Because he was a year older than me and almost twice as large, Ronny got the rubber and the picture. I got the letter. I don't remember what happened to it and remember only a couple of lines (**see those in bold italics**), but they still bring a smile to the small slice of ten year old still left in me. So, this is in homage to the American genius who wrote the original. It brought me great pleasure and improved my understanding of the world.

P.O. Box 666
Plainfield, NH, 04567
April 1, 2012

Benevolent Debt Recovery Corp.
10 Avarice Way
Secaucus, NJ, 12332

Dear sir:

I am writing in response to your letter of February 14 advising me that you will start legal action if I do not pay off my VISA credit card debt of $345,091.11 by April 15, 2012. I am in the hopes the information provided below may help you reevaluate your hostile course of action.

Only a few short years ago I was employed for 37 years in the HH&H Snath LLC in Plainfield, NH. In case you don't know what a snath is, it is the curved wooden handle attached to the long blade of a hay scythe. I always suspected the demand for snaths was slowed a bit with the advent of tractors and mowers. But, when the Chinese developed ergonomically advanced carbon fiber snaths distributed across the globe in Tractors R Us outlets for $9.95, it wasn't exactly a surprise when I was called to HR (that's Henry Reamer) given a ten dollar Timex watch and told I was retired.

Until then, I thought after 37 years, retirement was my call, but Henry reminded me that this was the US of A and with unions long gone, management could do whatever the hell it wanted. "So shut up and be thankful for the goddam watch." I then asked him to lay me off so I could collect unemployment. He said his father Hiram, the founder, didn't believe in Socialism.

When I returned to my desk, Security, yet another Reamer (Horace) was waiting for me to clear out my desk and get off the premises. As I was throwing my stuff in a box a few pictures of me in what you might call manly poses fell to the floor. I had brought them to work to use the digital scanner so I could email the pictures to an interesting interested woman in Omaha, Nebraska. Well! Old Horace just about croaked. When I got to my car he turned and shouted "See ya around Weiner." Now my name ain't Weiner but I knew all about that schmuck. I knew the whole town was going to snigger at me just like the whole country sniggered at Weiner.

That's when I lost it. I ran at old Horace and kicked him right in the shin. He went down real fast but so did I. I forgot he had a prosthetic leg from his stint in Vietnam. Worse yet I didn't even think about his being over 65. In just a few minutes I went from hard working solid citizen to jobless cheating porno creep felon who attacks elderly disabled war veterans. Oh yeah, and I broke my big toe. The judge gave me six months.

Actually, compared to working at HH&H, jail wasn't all that ba'd but the cold cell caused my prostate to act up. *So, for a while, all I did was wind my watch and piss.* Meanwhile my wife Sue went through our savings living off the VISA credit card. When I got out she didn't seem too happy to see me and I wasn't too happy to see a negative $45,000 VISA balance. Then my son Bob got kicked off the Plainfield High School football team for pouring a large barrel of Gatorade over Johnny Nimble the coach and Vice Principal. That might have been acceptable but not after a 42 -7 loss. I suspect he might have had anger issues. My son I mean.

Meanwhile my prostate got worse. I had no health insurance so I used VISA to buy tickets to India for one of those Mumbai surgery/vacation deals. The flight cost about $1,600 and the operation $29.95. As you may guess, I got what I paid for: a long flight including interesting little sugar coated anise seeds and an operation that leaves me impotent and in diapers for the rest of my life. To make matters worse, I discovered I had what you might call stomach issues about an hour into the flight back. Good thing I had the diapers but I still spent most of the time in the Boeing 747 toilet.

I guess Homeland Security figures that anyone who spends half a day in the toilet of a Boeing 747 has to be up to no good. When we landed I was escorted off the plane and held by Homeland Security for more than 48 hours. After a tough 15 hour flight they kept me up all night continually screaming at me to cut the shit and come clean. I still don't exactly know what they meant by that.

When I got back to New Hampshire, I got a registered letter from Sue informing me that she found real love and was moving to Ecuador with Consuela, our former cleaning lady. They planned to go off the grid, raise lamas, and give chocolate body massages to ex-pat baby boomers. I was worried sick that this was going to be a contentious expensive parting that neither of us could afford, but Sue said Ecuador would provide an inexpensive pathway to self-awareness and contentment. She asked for a one-time $20,000 payment in lieu of alimony. This sounded OK to me so I put the $20,000 on VISA.

Just when I thought things would settle down my son Bob put his fist through a window which cut arteries in his wrist. The admitting nurse had just ingested her nightly quota of Oxycontin. She took the wrong records, put an X on the wrong body part, put him on a gurney and shipped him off to the wrong floor of the hospital.

Actually the sex change operation went quite well but Bob was really pissed. I don't blame her. She had to get an entire new wardrobe. About a month later, I got a call from the NYC police that Barb was in Rikers Island on a charge of aggravated assault and poisoning pigeons. It turns out Barb auditioned for the Rockefeller Center Rockettes. The Rockette Casting Director told her that she couldn't high kick worth a damn (I mean who could with all those stitches). She said Barb looked like a football player and suggested she consider a sex change operation and learn to punt. The lawyer who specialized in transgender violence cases finally got Barb out on the condition she enter into anger management therapy— legal fees $26,000, therapy another $10,000.

I have many more stories, from failed brakes to rabid Ecuadorian iguanas, but I hope the narrative thus far adequately illustrates the trajectory of my recent life and the problems you may encounter in trying to squeeze even a dime out of me. In addition, while I have spent more than $77,000 on the VISA card, I owe more than $300,000 due to an interest rate of almost 20% per annum. This usurious rate profoundly challenges me to take your threat seriously. In sum, ***trying to get money out of me will be harder than shoving butter up a polecat's ass with a red hot poker.*** Thank you for your consideration.

Sincerely

Ingraham N. Payne

And, no. We never did return that wallet.

ANOTHER FAREWELL TO ARMS

The prompt for this story was for me to take Hemingway's opening page of *A Farewell to Arms,* and rewrite it:

"In the late summer of that year we lived in a house in a village that looked across the river and the plain to the mountains. In the bed of the river there were pebbles and boulders, dry and white in the sun, and the water was clear and swiftly moving and blue in the channels. Troops went by the house and down the road and the dust they raised powdered the leaves of the trees. The trunks of the trees too were dusty and the leaves fell early that year and we saw the troops marching along the road and the dust rising and leaves stirred by the breeze, falling and the soldiers marching and afterward the road bare and white except for the leaves."

- Earnest Hemingway, *A Farewell to Arms*

My rewrite

The troops march off leaving the dust to carry on. A handsome bearded man dressed in mufti clenches a worn notebook. He occasionally raises his eyes to look across the river to the village. The village bell tolls. It is then that we see the soldier—or better, what remains of him. He is carrying a box. A box recently painted white. It is tied to his back. He has no arms. The rope is clenched between his teeth. We cannot tell whether he's grimacing or smiling. We think the former. We are wrong.

He leaves the road, the road white except for the dusty leaves. He descends into the stream bed leaping from one white boulder to the next. The white box tied still to his back. We can see he's strong, agile. We can see he possesses that everyday courage for which we all yearn. He is a man—a manly man.

He comes to a halt on a boulder. Below him, the clear blue swiftly moving channel. He stands straight. Stands at attention. His lips move as if in prayer. He yanks on the knot with his teeth and bends forward with the speed and grace of a bull lion making a kill in the Serengeti. The box slides across his sweating back, a white blur in the blue air. Water hurls the box against the channel wall splitting it open offering up its contents. Two arms swirling, bobbing, wave in the rushing water, one hand clenched in a fist the other fingers extended in supplication. Two arms free from their owner, free from their white sepulcher, free to find their way to the sea. His lips still moving, the soldier once more bends at the waist only slowly now—an armless salute. His empty sleeves in the late summer breeze wave a feeble farewell.

We do not know much about death or what follows. But, we do know about dying. The thing is: it's how you do it. Even piece by piece, it's still how you do it.

TECHNOLOGIES

A Missed Opportunity

George first heard the rumble. It made him nervous but he had heard Noisegod and Wetgod many times before so he went back to tracking the rabbit. Suddenly the ground shook throwing him to the ground. He was terrified. The shaking became increasingly violent. The noise grew to a horrific pitch. He raised an arm and looked up. The entire mountain seemed to be falling. He tried to run but the ground was shaking too hard. George didn't see the large stone bouncing down the mountain at him. Angergod had come. Laying there paralyzed with fear, George pondered what he did to provoke Angergod. *What have I done? How can I appease him? How can I make it stop?* Prayer had not yet been invented.

Hours later George woke up still bleeding from a gash in the back of his head. Trembling and in shock, he tried to stand but had to kneel to steady himself. All was quiet. Then the earth gave a small last shiver and a clapping noise came from up the mountain. George couldn't move. He knelt there, waiting like the rabbits he caught. With eyes still glued to the mountain, he saw the stone tumbling down, rolling at him. It was the only thing moving, shedding small shards of granite as it bounced from rock to rock. George was familiar with death. He thought about rabbits. The stone came so fast, He didn't have time to raise his arms as the rolling stone hit a rock slab, sailed over his head, spun a few times, and fell flat to the ground. He stared at the stone. It was flat on both sides and strangely curved, a smooth continuous curve that explained why it rolled so far.

George was not sure Angergod had left but he crawled to the strange stone and carefully, softly felt the stone with his fingers. He tried to bite it. After more study, he concluded that the stone was not going to come after him; that it might be some sort of gift from Happygod. He decided to bring it home. After pushing it a few yards he found that if he kept it on its edge and pushed, he did not have to carry it. He could roll it although he had no word for "roll." Yet. No large stone was ever this easy to move.

For a Neanderthal, George was quite spiritual. He hoped Angergod would deliver another larger such stone so that he and his partner Martha could make an altar where the tribe could make larger sacrifices. *Angergod would be so pleased!* But Martha was half Homosapien. She had other ideas. She started to think about how to make flat stones round and use them for many, many uses. Today she would be called an early adaptor.

Fire

According to anthropologist, Polly Wiessner, 400,000 years ago when our ancestors learned to control fire, the quality of their lives changed dramatically. Besides helping them scare off saber-tooth tigers, keep warm, and grill some wicked wooly mammoth steaks, our brain and gut size increased. Why did fire make us smarter and fatter? Because, FIRELIGHT introduced LEISURE TIME! We could now stay up late and PARTY!

We became more civilized. At night we had time to think. During the day our conversation was limited to immediate economic concerns such as "Look! A bear! Who got the spear?" or, "OK! Who stole my nuts?" But at night, talk was about the past and the future. "Daddy, did Grandpa Og really fly? Will we ever get to the moon?" Things like that.

HEAD HUNTED

This is the first story I ever wrote from a South Kingstown Rhode Island Guild Writing Group prompt. That first prompt is a story in itself. Back then, the Guild Writing Group was in transition between the time Betty Carter left and a new leader Apphia Duey had yet to start. So for a few weeks, the inmates ran the asylum. When it came time to choose a prompt, Davis Fogg suggested cannibals. Now this is my first Guild meeting and I'm wondering what the hell am I getting into. I mean here's a guy with the moniker of C. Davis Fogg (that's right Fogg with two Gs) telling me I had to write a story about cannibals—first time out of the gate just because he hung out with cannibals one time .

As it turns out Davis had spent time in Africa in the Peace Corps. not too far from a tribe still practicing cannibalism. This generated a bit of discussion from which I learned that the members of that tribe referred to white men as long pigs and that the members of the Guild Writing Group collectively were brilliant negotiators. They expanded the cannibal prompt to include "head hunters." Well hell! That's all I needed. I wrote a story. I even had fun writing it. So the next time you get stuck on a gnarly prompt, write about cannibals or head hunters. This is my story.

Lou De Luca looked out the window as he usually did when he needed a lift. He could see Staten Island from his office. He could almost see his home and the neighborhood where he grew up. This view of the financial center of the world never failed to restore his spirits. He even had the office name ELITE EXECUTIVE SEARCH, LLC etched on the window to remind him of how far he had come. Today Lou definitely needed a lift. Things in the company were changing—changing fast. Mostly it was the foreign competition. But the new boss also had new ideas: rearranging the organization, pushing into new markets, taking on risky jobs, rolling over old allies. The boss called it the new global paradigm whatever the hell that was. Lou called it nuts.

Like today waiting for a return call from a reference in Sri Lanka. Sri Lanka! Where the hell is that? Colombo! Isn't that a yogurt place over by Hell's Kitchen? And me, almost a Fordham graduate. Lou played two years at right tackle before dropping out. He loved to knock guys down, knock guys out! But that was a long time ago. Now Lou resented the flab that had once been muscle, the reading glasses, hearing aids, knee replacement, Viagra. He wasn't sure where he started or ended any more. The sharp buzz of the intercom interrupted Lou's silent elegy.

"Mr. D, a Mr. Premadasa from Sri Lanka returning your call on line 2."

"Hello Mr. Premadasa. Hey! Thanks for returning my call. We are about to engage in a far reaching reorganization and are looking for a top tier professional to help us execute our plan. I was told you have a guy, Sam, who has an impressive resume and a record of completing difficult tasks in a timely manner."

"Oh! yes, I am knowing Sam very well indeed. But, I must tell you Mr. De Luca, that Samika is not a 'guy' as you say. She is, however, a very interesting lady. She has worked in many countries in very important engagements in the public as well as the private sector. I am not knowing anyone who was not most pleased with her work. I would be recommending her most highly."

After a half hour on the phone Lou thanked Mr. Premadasa and started putting together his report for the boss. He knew better than to add his two cents *that hiring a broad for this assignment was without a doubt just plain nuts.*

Two weeks later Lou was again staring out the window when the intercom interrupted his late afternoon uplifting reverie.

"Mr. De Luca, a Ms. Samika is here to see you."

Lou turned in surprise. What the hell was this Samika broad doing here now?

The force of the large caliber bullet lifted Lou through his much loved window. The Company reorg was underway.

LAUGHTER RANT

The thing of it is his laugh. It warms the room. Folks want a piece of it especially at noisy parties where you can't hear a goddam thing folks are saying. To make matters worse, they seem to always lower their voice when they get to the punchline, like a conspiracy or something. Ever notice that? Ever notice that folks listening, laugh even though they can't hear the punch line or don't have a clue to what it means. You can tell from their puny little timid laughs, Hehhehheh. Although, not all bogus laughs are puny. In fact, some are real loud. They have what I call the Nazi machine gun laugh. Like the guy has an AK47 or something stuck in his mouth. "HAHAHAHA."

One of the funniest jokes I ever heard was in the army by a guy who claimed he went to Harvard. I had my doubts about that Harvard stuff but he talked a lot about "ugly Cliffies" at Harvard's sister school back then and he sure could tell a joke. After a solid hour of rattling off nonstop funny stuff, he turned the tables and says he forgot how a particular joke went but remembers the punch line. "Does anyone know the joke that goes with the punchline. "Well, tally ho, men! I'll stick mine in the mash potatoes!" Hey! …maybe you had to be there.

But anyway, it doesn't matter. Most jokes are lame. They insult people on both ends of the socioeconomic scale. Hey! How do you like that? … You know, this "socioeconomic scale" crap. I bet that surprised you. I bet you had me figured for a high school dropout or something, just looking for a free drink. Hey! I did finish high school, but, it wasn't easy. My mom died when I was 14. Overdosed on Molly at a rave no less. Man she could ball. Haven't seen my sister in almost two years. Still in Rikers I guess.

See that bearded guy by the entrance with those three hotties hanging all over him? That's my brother. I mean my big brother. He's got a great big laugh. This is his show. That's all his work hanging on the walls here. I can't believe people buy this shit. I think it's his laugh. Makes folks feel that they're part of the art scene, part of the "Elite" art clan. I suspect that by the time they get home, they're saying "What the fuck was I thinking?"

I once told my brother, if he lived like he laughed, he'd be one happy sonofabitch. Instead he's one miserable, conniving, perfect sonofabitch. But, you know, I sure wish I could laugh like that. I might even start painting. I'd be laughing all the way to the bank. Can I get you another drink? They're free you know.

The Everlasting Season

James and Jackie on Santa's lap. Circa 1984.

Max stepped behind the dressing room door and took a nip from a small fake silver flask hidden in his thick winter coat. He liked the feel of that flask. It was a 14th birthday gift from his younger brother long gone these many years. Max heaved a heavy sigh, took off his coat and let it drop to the floor. Stripping to his undershirt he slowly lowered his sunburned face into a thin graying towel.

Jesus! Lunchtime and I'm already soaked. This Goddam beard itches like hell, and now a new rash between my legs. What the hell was I thinking? I was pretty good in the old days. Kids laughing, everyone happy. How can I make anyone happy now when my boots are slowly filling with my own sweat. Great! That's really gonna help my athlete's foot. Some athlete I am! And this beard, it smells like a dead rat. At least the brats don't seem to mind and the moms they're smart. Keep their distance. Last thing they want to do is sit on my lap.

Why did I tell them, "Yeah, if I can do winter, I can do it summer. Piece of cake! Right! Besides, I'll make enough to get out of that pay-by-the-week Motel Six rat hole—maybe even score a little meth. Invite Lucy. Yeah.

Max was not much surprised that aside from the various rashes ravaging his body, Christmas in July never went viral—at least not here in Arizona. In a way he was glad, but the utter and complete failure of a prior Christmas in July initiative caused him serious problems, problems like food, shelter, addictions, and his inability to keep from scratching his crotch—even in public. Being Santa was all he knew, was all he was good at. Now he was reduced to panhandling outside WalMart. He noticed that the WalMart Greeter job wasn't much different than his old Santa gig so he applied for a job as a WalMart greeter.

Max was not aware that WalMart had made a corporate decision to arm all greeters with Glock 47s in order to reduce an escalating number of assaults in their parking lots and men's rooms. A handful of felonies kept Max from packing any heat in WalMart. He was cleaning up for the day in a WalMart men's room when the idea hit him.

Jesus! Why didn't I think of this before. Christmas on Halloween! This will even be bigger than those goddam Creepy Clown Masks that make cops nervous and little brats whimper. Target got rid of some of their masks but they ain't fooling no one. They're still making a killing on Kiddie Clown, Sexy Clown, Playboy Clown, and all that crap!

Max worried a bit that Christmas on Halloween might confuse those WalMart shoppers who either didn't know that Christmas is in December or didn't know what month they were currently in. But, that did not deter Max. He knew he was onto something big. He popped a Deltoid breath mint, took a deep breath, smiled his best Santa smile and headed for the WalMart manager's office. Stumbling out into the blinding July Arizona sun, Max popped another Deltoid, smiled his best smile and shouted whiskey voiced into the shimmering blackness of an empty Dollar Store parking lot "Ho! Ho! Ho! Merry Christmas!"

What was I thinking?

18

HEAVEN & HELL

HOLY SMOKE

Every Sunday afternoon, Saint Michael's parish in Hartford, Connecticut celebrated the Rite of Eucharistic Exposition and Benediction. This rite requires a priest, two altar boys, lots of smoke, and some chanting. The purpose of the exposition is to take the Host from its usual place in the Tabernacle and put it in a real fancy container called a "solar" monstrance. This monstrance is then shown (exposed) to those faithful enough to use up some of their weekend kneeling and watch the Host transubstantiate into bread (the body of Christ) and wine (the blood of Christ).

The priest then eats the bread which is actually a thin tasteless wafer and drinks the wine. No matter how diligent, me and my altar boy partner Ned never seem to get a chance to see any of this transubstantiation stuff. After a few Sunday Benediction gigs, Ned and I begin to think maybe there is no transubstantiation, and, even if there was, wouldn't devouring a real body and real blood make us and the priest cannibals or vampires or something even cooler?

One Sunday afternoon Ned and I draw benediction duty again. Even as believers we're pretty crummy altar boys. We often forgot important steps in rituals and we never ever got the hang of Latin. Several weeks earlier, Ned got a little confused serving Father Bannon at mass and poured wine not water over Father Bannon's fingers into the little washbowl and poured water instead of wine into the shiny gold chalice.

The good news was that Father Bannon didn't skip a beat. For him, the show must go on. The bad news was that Father Bannon didn't like kids, especially poor kids even though he was principal of our grammar school. He would have been much happier as President of the Rich Ladies Soft Priest Society or something.

Anyway, because Ned can no longer be trusted, I'm given the task of dealing with the incense burner even though I never messed with it before. It has all these chains and by the time it's ready for the priest to shake the incense burner over the monstrance, the charcoal is already pretty hot. I pull one of the chains to open the top cover so the priest can sprinkle a few spoonfuls of incense onto the charcoal. With the addition of the incense, things are getting real hot. Languorous smoke curls up. All in all it's beautiful. I'm transfixed.

Father Bannon gives me a quiet cough. This means it's time to put the top cover back on. I look at the chain I had used to lift the cover. It's just laying there... flaccid. It must be one of the other chains but which one and how do I work the sonofabitch anyway. I'm thinking along these lines as the folks in the church start to cough in polite impatience. You know, one guy coughs, and all of a sudden it sounds like a choir of sick hackers just snuck in. At this point, all folks want to do is sing the "Tantum Ergo," chant the "Devine Praises," and head home to Sunday supper. Father Bannon, afraid the show might come to a halt, grabs the top of the incense burner. Maybe it's my imagination, but I swear I can still hear the sizzle. Father Bannon starts fiddling with the chains. They're all screwed up. He's all screwed up. He gives me a look then looks out over the congregation, spreads his arms, smiles and starts in on the "Tantum Ergo" I breathe a sigh of relief. Thank God!

When Benediction is over we leave the altar from the opposite side we came in on. We walk ahead of the priest back to the first side where garments are changed. Father Bannon unhooks the clasp from his Benediction cape (we Catholics call it a cope), and, with the speed and elegance of great matador Manolete he throws the cape over my head and starts swinging the incense burner at me. It was a close call—I never got hurt. I think the cape saved me, but this was probably the beginning of my slow loss of faith and my descent into hell.

HEY ZEUS

Jesus in Ecuador. Circa 2017.

"Dumb birds! I don't mind the pigeons but condors. Talk about guano! Thank god for the thorns! That'll keep those condors off the roof."

Hey Zeus stood on the dome of the basilica one arm reaching for clouds playing atop the Andes mountains, the other beckoning to the people of Cotacachi in Ecuador. He loved it here, up so high, more than twenty-five feet tall, watching all the little people come to the church although he didn't know why they came or what exactly they did there. They were very polite to him though, tipping their hats, bowing, sometimes just looking up at him moving their lips and crying. For some reason even though they were so small, it made him feel warm. He loved the singing especially when the children sung. He wished he knew the words but no matter how many times he heard a tune he could never figure out what they were singing about.

Every now and then the little people would leave the church and march around the town square. Hey Zeus looked forward to this because the little men would carry a statue of a beautiful woman in a blue robe. As much as he enjoyed the marching and dancing and the band he sometimes felt lonely. He wondered just how many other statues existed. Might there be a statue of another beautiful woman but closer to his size?

Sometimes instead of the beautiful woman statue the men carried a baby boy statue. Everyone smiles. They throw coins at the baby statue. Hey Zeus worried that the coins would chip and hurt the little boy. He wondered if the baby would ever grow up. How big would he get? Would he be able to understand the little people? It was a lot to ponder.

A BIG MISTAKE

I dunno! Maybe it's all a big mistake. It sounded so good when I started out. Of course my son thought I was nuts. But then, what else is new. He was against it right from the start. Thought I was just bored. But give him credit. Although he didn't agree with the plan, when things went south, he did make a valiant effort to straighten out the mess. Talk about blood, sweat, and tears! But now, it looks like it just made things worse. In fact, much worse. So many folks claim their big book has all the answers and folks who think otherwise deserve to die—especially unarmed women and children.

After all the gifts I gave them, after all the sacrifices my son made, these folks have become self-destructive lunatics. It seems they ruin or misuse every damn thing I give them (pardon my French). They're hell bent on destroying the earth and destroying each other. Worse yet, they do all kinds of terrible things in my name. For some reason they think I just sit around listening to their special requests and as part of the deal I seek their adoration and an occasional candle. They keep asking for forgiveness. Really? Forgive? Give me a break! They think I look like them right down to the scratchy beards and strange little belly buttons. OK, OK, The bellybuttons were my idea. I thought they were kinda cute. So do teenage boys.

Bucket Lists

Virgin Mary's Bucket List

Ask Jesus to call me and his father every now and then
Keep the angel Gabriel out of my life
Put a little spine in Joseph
Find out what The Holy Ghost has been up to lately
Look into birth control
Become a priest

Jesus's Bucket List

Try another Last Meal, this time from Blue Apron
Plead nolo to Original Sin
Pardon Pontius Pilot
Try a man bun
Get Mary Magdalene a nice pair of Birkenstocks
Find out what The Holy Ghost has been up to lately

Holy Ghost Bucket List

Move to Williamsburg, Brooklyn
Wear black
Wear a mask
Try to remember exactly what I have been up to lately
Write a memoir

Steve Bannon's Bucket List

Read Ayn Rand sober
Get a small bowl to catch trickle-down economics

An Early Lesson

My first encounters with death didn't amount to much. I went to my 88-year-old grandmother's wake but being only five, I was not allowed (or forced) to go in the big room and look at her. Instead they put me in a room filled with men smoking pipes and cigarettes and nipping from silver flasks snugged in the inside pocket of their Sunday suits.

No one could find my father in time to attend his mother's funeral so my mother took us by train from Hartford, Connecticut to Springfield, Massachusetts. I think my mother was seen as what back then was called a grass widow—a woman temporarily without a husband at home. In hindsight, this grass widow status of my mother stirred wishful thinking among the men, which, in turn stirred some interest in me. "So boyo! Yer from Hartford? Eh? You going to take care of yer mammy like the stout lad? Eh? Keep all those dagoes and coons off her. Eh?" "Paud! For Chrissake! Let the lad alone. You're no better than his goddam father." I finally did get closer to death on one of our Sunday visits to the Murphy's. They lived a couple of blocks from the Fuller Brush Factory. The factory looked like a seminary but, instead of pumping out priest to cleanse our souls, the Fuller Brush Company sent legions of Fuller Brush Men door to door to cleanse our bodies.

I always looked forward to the two mile Sunday afternoon walk to the Murphy's. I liked to play with Maryellen and Eamon who we called Yeman. Another brother, Brendan, was too old to bother with us. I liked to hear my mother speaking Gaelic. I liked to hear her laugh with her friends. Mike Murphy, the father, was a big man with big rough hands who worked on the railroad. He always gave me a big hug. His whiskers scratched. I wasn't used to grown men and not sure whether or not I liked it, though.

I did like it when he played Santa on Christmas. His suit and fake beard were pretty cheesy, but it was his voice that clinched it. Even his "Ho! Ho! Ho!" had a brogue. I suspect this adult deception of Santa planted the first seeds of atheism in me.

Like Jesus, Brendan was a carpenter except that he married a fancy model and moved to a fancy apartment in Manhattan. He always gave the doorman a big "Good Morning!" as he left for work with lunch pail in hand. He also was a very good motorcycle racer. He was killed racing on the Isle of Man—one of the more than two hundred deaths claimed by that race over the past hundred years. Brendan's wife had him cremated on the Isle of Man. I'm not sure where the ashes ended up but the whole deal didn't sit well with the very Catholic Murphy family. From that day on, big Mike Murphy sat in his recliner getting up only to relieve himself. He just stared out the window, maybe trying to see his old home in Ireland or perhaps the Isle of Man beyond. I don't know what he saw but it was not us.

Brendan's death came long after my first introduction with death. The Murphy's house abutted a golf course. We would crawl under the fence and, barefoot, run on what was to us city kids a perfect lawn that went forever. On this particular day the fairways were being mowed by a tractor pulling an array of reel mowers that cut a 20 foot swath. We hid when the tractor came around.

On one of the rounds, the mower scared up a family of rabbits. They ran in all directions. We saw a baby rabbit get flipped in the air behind the mower. Maryellen, a couple of years older than us, got to it first. She named it Baby Rabbit. With that, she owned it. I was jealous even though Baby Rabbit might not hop so good anymore. It was not much bigger than a field mouse. Baby Rabbit's chest rose and fell, its little heart beating a hundred miles an hour. Part of Baby Rabbit's leg was missing. I remember the pearly whiteness of the bone sticking out where the leg should have been. No blood, no crying, just staring, it's little heart beating away. But, we were going to fix Baby Rabbit. Make her all better.

Mary Ellen carried Baby Rabbit home. Yeman found a little box for her. I don't know why Maryellen knew it was a girl, but, girl or boy, we picked the greenest grass we could find and made a loving nest in that box. Yeman then got a bottle cap for drinking water. We talked about going back to find the leg. Maryellen said that was stupid "you can't just glue a leg back on a baby rabbit. They're too young." Although I resented Maryellen's know-it-all stuff, I was kind of glad we didn't have to go look for Baby Rabbit's leg. I was afraid I would find it. Then what?

Yeman was now looking for a place to house Baby Rabbit. We had saved it from the mower but somehow knew we also had to save it from the adults. We laid an old towel across the top of the box. Just then, Brendan, who was included in the adult category, came around the corner of the house. "What's in the box Maryellen?"

Turning her back to Brendan. "Nothing."

"C'mon now Maryellen what is it?"

"Just a little bunny."

By now Brendan is looking into the box. "Oh! Poor little thing. He's a goner!"

Maryellen pulled the box tight to her chest. "He…. She is not no goner! We are going to save her and keep her."

"Bull shit!"

Coming from the almost adult twelve year old, these two words started my heart beating. Beating like Baby Rabbit's. She's a goner? Where will she go?

Brendan grabbed the box from Maryellen and marched into the house carrying it like a priest carrying Jesus under that cloth at mass. A short time later Mike came out, got a pail from the shed, and disappeared around the house. He returned to the back yard and threw what looked like a wet glove over the fence onto the green fairway. Maryellen started wailing. Mike came over and patted her on the shoulder. She pulled away, pointed her finger at him and screamed something I didn't understand. This got her a swift slap on the rear and sent to bed. We left soon after. Looking back, I didn't know then why my mother was mad at us or why I was mad at Baby Rabbit. It's hard to understand grownups sometimes.

LAST STORY

This essay was written at the request of good friend Al Killilea who published a book containing essays from more than one hundred people addressing the question: "In the face of death, how do you find meaning and fulfillment in life?" The essays were limited to 250 words or less.

Given the bizarre self-serving pictures man-made religion paints of the afterlife, it looks to me like this life is the only game in town. (I do pray I'm wrong.) So, if this life is all I got and death is the final act, I'll opt for a slow mortification of the flesh. This will give me an opportunity to show my kids how to die right, like Mimi in *La bohème*, singing a beautiful aria while dying of consumption. Other possibilities include: getting hit by a bus; dying while saving nuns from a burning church;

or, as projected for me, forgetting who I am. Today is March 22, 2020. It's beginning to look like the coronavirus might just do the trick. So I'll keep using a mask, washing my hands, and hoping for a soft and timely landing.

As a spiritually limited atheist, I suspect the desire to do good is a Darwinian tribal survival trait. It would be great to be admired. Unfortunately I've run out of time to discover the cure for cancer or to create a bumper sticker that will bring peace in our time. So the best I can hope for is a legacy that influences my kids and maybe future grandkids for the good of the tribe. A small ripple of values across a few years. Not so great. Eh? But as Harriet McBryde Johnson, a wheelchair bound advocate for the disabled said, "When I die, I might as well die alive." That's the plan. I know life laughs at our plans but if the world is a better place for my being part of it, I'm good to go.

250 words to summarize my eschatological existence. Jesus! I haven't died yet so what the hell do I know about it.

ABOUT THE AUTHOR

I was born in Hartford, Connecticut on what was then Armistice Day, November 11, 1941, and baptized on December 7, 1941, the day Pearl Harbor was attacked. I was named John Barry after my father (but I've always preferred to go by 'Jack'). John Barry also happened to be the name of the real Father of the American Navy. Later, in the Army, I often pondered that militaristic beginning, for, just as with so many young men going off to serve their country, I was no warrior. I was also no lover, much to my despair at the time.

After finishing my two-year stint in the army, pure dumb luck and perfect timing gave me an opportunity to participate in the birth of the revolution in information technology. This revolution was fueled by Moore's Law which states that overall processing power for computers doubles every two years.

In 1966 I applied to the Connecticut General Life Insurance Company for a Computer Operator night shift position in order to attend UCONN as a student. After an interview at Connecticut General, they scheduled some tests, after which they offered me a Programmer position. Meanwhile the UCONN folks told me I would have to take courses at the Storrs campus for the first two years. Given the awesome annual salary of $4,500, it was an easy decision. And, I never did get a degree. My career path reflected the opportunities created by the IT revolution. Major positions included:

Connecticut General Life Insurance Company, Computer Programmer;

Dartmouth College, Systems Analyst;

University of Rhode Island, Director of The Administrative Computer Center, and Director of Network and Telecommunications.

Made in the USA
Middletown, DE
21 December 2021

54406399R00119